Start Here:

A Crash Course in Understanding, Navigating, and Healing from Narcissistic Abuse

Dana Morningstar

D1059935

Copyright © 2017 by Dana Morningstar
All rights reserved. This book or any portion thereof
may not be reproduced or used in any manner whatsoever
without the express written permission of the publisher
except for the use of brief quotations in a book review.
Printed in the United States of America
First Printing, 2017
Morningstar Media
PO Box 464

Mason, MI 48854

For my Grandmother, Mildred Morningstar, a woman who went through hell and came out even stronger. You are my hero and a huge inspiration.

Acknowledgements

A special thank you to the administrators and volunteers who help run the support groups, the book club, the live streams, and tech support. Words don't even come close to expressing how thankful and grateful I am for all of your hard work and continued support of me and all the other members of this community. You are beyond appreciated and greatly valued.

Disclaimer

This book is not intended to treat or diagnose anyone. It is intended to be a solid starting point for those going through any type of "confusing," "crazy-making," or otherwise toxic or abusive relationship or situation. If you take one thing away from this book it is that while the labels (diagnoses) can be helpful and validating, they are perhaps best understood as pointers to problematic behavior. And while the labels and diagnoses change over time, the behaviors they point to do not.

Table of Contents

Introduction

This book is a compilation of terms, concepts, and aha moments I've gained through my own journey of understanding and healing from narcissistic abuse, much of which has come from talking to others who have been through similar experiences.

The goal of this book is to provide a crash course to understanding narcissistic abuse. What you will find in here is an overview of the most common questions, concepts, comments, concerns, frustrations, and confusion regarding narcissistic abuse in general.

My hope is that this book, as well as any of my other material can guide you to the clarity and understanding that you are looking for so that you can move forward into all the healing and happiness possible.

And I think a lot is possible.

If you'd like to join our community or have any questions, comments, concerns, frustrations, feedback, you can find me at: www.ThriveAfterAbuse.com where you can also find all the details about the support group, book club, weekly Q&A and support live stream, podcast episodes, other books I'm working on and much more.

Who This Book is For

Every month I interact with hundreds of different people either through email or in my support group, and I've come to realize that there are three main groups of people that I come across: clarity seekers, support or strategy seekers, or support or strategy givers.

- Clarity seekers are those seeking insight into what they are experiencing.

- Support or strategy seekers are those who have clarity about what they are experiencing, and who are now seeking support and strategies on how to cope with and/or heal from it.

- Support and strategy givers are those who want to better understand the topic of narcissistic abuse from a survivor's perspective so they can better help a friend, family member, or client.

I think it's important to address each of these three types of people, as I think you will find it helpful in validating how you may feel (especially if you are a clarity seeker).

The clarity seeker knows something is "off" in their relationship but feels lost in a fog of confusion and self-doubt, and may not be able to pinpoint who has the problem or what the problem even is. They might even be in therapy but still feel like something is missing. Because of this, they are finding themselves stuck in a mental loop of continually questioning what they are experiencing and who has the problem. They may be wondering if they are too sensitive, emotional, jealous, insecure, needy, or distrusting, or if their partner is the one who is insensitive, rude, lying, manipulative, or cheating. They may be trying everything under the sun to get through to their partner just how hurtful their behavior is and may be frustrated that no matter what they say, their partner never seems to change for long. All they know for sure is that they feel emotionally blown apart and exhausted by their relationship.

They might have even come across the terms "narcissist," "sociopath," or "psychopath" which seem to fit a lot of what they are experiencing, but it might feel harsh or extreme to call this person any of those names—or they want to know for sure that this person is indeed personality disordered before they consider walking away.

They may fear that maybe this person really is a "normal" person who just has a lot of problematic behavior, possibly because of their childhood—maybe they were spoiled or maybe they claimed to have been abused (and maybe they really were), or perhaps they had a "crazy" ex who cheated or abused them. Then comes the inevitable hope that given enough love, understanding, support, therapy, rehab, or religion this person could change, and together they could have this amazing relationship…if only they hang in there long enough for the change to happen. After all, the good times are so good…but the bad times are so bad.

Or perhaps the clarity seeker has been told for so long that they are somehow the problem—that they are manipulative, abusive, crazy, too emotional, too sensitive, too jealous, too insecure, or even that *they* are the narcissist and have manipulative, abusive, mentally ill, or "crazy" behavior. And after hearing this for so long, they are confused and fearful that maybe they really are the problem.

Start Here

Oftentimes clarity seekers start off describing their experience with something like, "I know this sounds crazy but..." "I'm scared I might be a narcissist..." "I'm not sure if he (or she) is really a narcissist, but they lie/cheat/steal/manipulate/are abusive..." "I'm embarrassed to tell you this, but..." "What if I'm the problem?"

The second type of person is the support or strategy seeker. Generally, this person's relationship has recently ended, or they are wanting it to end, and they are looking for answers, a plan, or support. Once they came across some information about narcissism, they were able to get the validation and clarity that they were looking for and everything began to make sense. Odds are this person is here looking to better understand some of the terminology that they've heard floating around (such as "flying monkeys," "narcissistic abuse," "reactive abuse," "gaslighting," and projection"), and they are here for strategies and support on how to break free emotionally or physically from this person.

The third type of person is a support and strategy giver. They are either a friend, family member, or clinician/law enforcement/attorney/spiritual leader (or student in the psychology, social work, counseling, criminal justice, law enforcement, or religious studies field) who is looking to better understand the topic of narcissistic abuse from those that have "been there, done that." They might be struggling with how to best support a loved one who either continues to go back to a "problematic" partner or has left but seems to be stuck in either anger, depression, or in reliving the abuse. The support and strategy giver wants to help but doesn't know how. Everything they've tried so far makes their loved one avoid them or lash out in anger.

Chapter 1: I'm Not Sure

I Belong Here

If you are like most people who have been in some sort of "problematic" or "crazy-making" dynamic for any length of time, you may feel really confused about what happened (or is happening) and uncertain if this person was the best thing to happen to you or the worst thing to happen to you—or if what you are experiencing falls within the realm of "normal" relationship problems. You may find yourself wondering how you got into a relationship like this in the first place, why you feel so "addicted" to them, or why no one understands or is able to support you. You may have stopped telling friends and family about what goes on during the bad times, because they are horrified—but in your mind this is normal for your relationship, and because you didn't want to leave—but didn't want to be lectured, you quit reaching out. If your relationship recently ended, you may feel incredibly lonely, ground down, enraged, overwhelmed, scared, anxious, depressed, numb, and overall physically and emotionally exhausted—like you are one hundred years old.

And if you do go back, you will most likely find yourself "forgetting" or glossing over much of their bad behavior and instead holding onto the fond memories of all the good times—and it's those good times that pull you back into contacting them again—hoping that maybe this time things really will be different. But no matter what they promise, they never seem to change for good—if anything, their behavior gets worse, or they get better at hiding what they've been up to, and when their double life comes to the surface, you are blamed for all of their lying, cheating, controlling, manipulating, or abuse that follows!

And perhaps after going through this cycle a few times, you decided to turn to the internet in hopes of making sense of what you were experiencing. Odds are you came across some videos on YouTube on narcissism or narcissistic abuse and things began to make sense, but you aren't sure if the person is really a narcissist (especially if they seemed really likable, nice, humble, charitable, or apologetic), or if what you experienced is really narcissistic abuse (especially if you were never called names, yelled at, or abused in any outright way).

If they left you, you may wonder if you'll ever trust people, let alone love again—especially if they moved on at lightning speed and seem so happy with their new partner, while you are left to sort through all the emotional (and usually financial) devastation that they left behind—including all their lies and acting as if they are a victim of you—and what's worse, is if people (including your friends, family, and children) believe them, because after all, they come across as so sympathetic and convincing while you come across as an anxious, angry, confused mess.

All of this confusion, all of these emotions are very normal, and my hope is that by the end of this book you will have a lot more clarity about your situation, as well as the next few steps to take.

And odds are if you are like most of us who have gone through this journey of understanding and healing, you will continue to have questions. At times you might feel as if you've entered the movie "The Matrix" where you are starting to see the world around you (and the people in it) clearly—perhaps for the first time ever.

Chapter 2: What Is a Narcissist and What Is a Personality Disorder?

What is a narcissist?

According to the Diagnostic and Statistical Manual of Mental Disorders, 5th edition, a person with Narcissistic Personality Disorder (NPD) is someone who has an inflated sense of self-worth, or of their abilities; someone who needs admiration and approval of others, has an impaired ability to empathize with others—or is excessively attuned to the reactions of others if there is benefit to them, has relationships that are superficial and self-serving, and continually strives to be the center of attention.

However, I think it's important to also bring up the topic of Antisocial Personality Disorder (ASPD) (formerly known as "sociopaths" or "psychopaths"), as there is overlap between the two. While not all narcissists are sociopaths or psychopaths, all sociopaths or psychopaths are narcissists at the core. Some key traits of ASPD behavior is a lack of concern for feelings, needs, or suffering of others, a disregard for rules and laws, exploitation and manipulation as their primary way of relating to others, and the use of dominance and intimidation to control others.

What is a personality disorder?

A personality disorder is a pervasive and persistent way of acting that negatively impacts a person's relationships or their ability to function in society—regardless of whether or not they realize it. In terms of narcissists and antisocials, they tend to have a pattern of using, abusing, exploiting, manipulating or neglecting others in order to get what they want.

For those of us who have been on the receiving end of this behavior, their behavior is often described as: controlling, immature, crazy-making, psycho, abusive, predatory, charming or charismatic, intense, persistent (especially when they are trying to worm their way back into their target's life), dark, sinister, evil, toxic, demonic, delusional, or terrifying. They often come across with a staggering lack of accountability, a jaw-dropping level of indifference to the hurt and heartache they cause, and a blinding degree of selfishness. They are usually pathological liars (and usually cheaters), highly manipulative, and in short, emotional vampires.

In short, narcissists are all about themselves—often at the expense of others. They do whatever they want, with whomever they want, as much as they want, and they feel entitled and justified in doing so—and they will often say or do anything they need to in order to keep their emotional con game going so they can continue to use, abuse, or exploit their target(s).

Many people get stuck at this point, wanting to know if the problematic person in their life does in fact have a personality disorder, or if they "just" have persistently problematic behavior. Frankly, however, either way you cut it, it's highly problematic and worthy of being a deal breaker. So while getting a diagnosis that this problematic person in your life does indeed have a personality disorder can be very validating, what's more important is that you are able to discern what toxic behavior is to you and then to respond accordingly. In many ways, trying to figure out to what degree their behavior is toxic to you is a lot like trying to figure out what kind of poison you've been drinking. At the end of the day it doesn't really matter; if it's strychnine, arsenic, or cyanide, what matters is toxic is toxic and to distance yourself as much as possible from it.

Chapter 3: What Exactly Is

Narcissistic Abuse?

Narcissistic abuse is where a narcissist targets and manipulates someone into giving up their wants, needs, feelings (and thus their identity) in order for the narcissist to get their self-esteem needs met.

The concept of narcissistic abuse was studied by psychoanalysts Sándor Ferenczi and Karen Horney, and later in the work of psychologist, Alice Miller. Their work primarily focused on exploring the family dynamics between a narcissistic parent (or parents) and their children. What Miller found in her work with emotionally abused and neglected children was that in order for them to "survive" their environment (meaning, in order for them to try to get their basic needs met—including food, clothing, shelter, love, and acceptance), they were forced to give up their own wants, needs, and feelings--and thus their identity in order to serve their parent's need for validation and esteem.

The term "narcissistic abuse" has since grown to include any dynamic (such as a "friend," parent, child, neighbor, coworker, significant other, member of their church, etc.) between a narcissist and their "target" to where the target is manipulated out of their wants and needs, and thus their sense of self in order to please or satisfy the other.

If you've experienced narcissistic abuse, the above-mentioned definition might feel like it pales in comparison to what you've gone through. But keep reading. The following chapter on definitions and the cycle of narcissistic abuse gives examples of what narcissistic abuse looks like in motion.

In addition to understanding what narcissistic abuse is, it's also critical to make two additional connections. The first is how another person is manipulated into giving up their own wants and needs, and the second is what drives this narcissistically-abusive behavior.

A target is manipulated through a series of boundary pushes that, over time, erode a person's sense of reality along with their sense of self. This "grinding down" happens slowly and systematically through some form of abusive or neglectful behavior. This includes any type (or combination of) verbal, emotional, psychological, physical, sexual, financial, or spiritual abuse. What drives abusive behavior is the need for a narcissistic person to get and keep power and control over another (so that they can continue to meet their own esteem needs).

It's also important to realize that these boundary erosions are primarily done in isolation (what happens at home stays at home), evolve in a slow and steady way and are often minimized or denied by the abusive person. The abuser often blames the target for being the cause for treating them this way. Narcissists grind others down in such a way that the target doesn't realize it until much later, and it's done in such a way that they feel like they are letting the narcissist down and deserve to be treated this way.

This erosion of another person's sense of self is generally done in four main ways:

1. **Slow and subtle.** This is where a person is continually being undermined and their faith in their decision-making abilities and reality as a whole is slowly being erased. This happens when one person continually tells another that they are some form of wrong, bad, or incompetent. What makes this form of abuse so dangerous (and effective) is that sometimes there is a kernel of truth to what the other person is saying, and it can even come across as though they are concerned about the person they are grinding down. This results in a person having a hard time developing the self-esteem needed in order to set goals and achieve them. They get caught up in self-doubt or worse, self-loathing. They often turn to the abusive person for guidance because the abusive person seems so certain as to what they should do or how they should feel. When a person is continually told that they are too sensitive, too emotional, jealous, controlling, manipulative, or flat-out crazy whenever they have an issue with a narcissist's hurtful, rude, provoking, controlling, manipulative, or crazy-making behavior, they are often left with not knowing who has the problem—if it's them or if it's the abuser.

2. **Fast and not so subtle.** This is when the use of direct intimidation and aggression is used to gain power and control over someone. This could be yelling, cussing, throwing something at the victim, or throwing something in general, hitting a wall, hitting them, or any other act that is intimidating or violent. This kind of behavior tends to happen fast and out of the blue and for seemingly no reason. Within an instant, the dy-

namic of the relationship has changed, and the target has now learned to never question them, challenge them, or act in any way that might upset them.

3. **Hot and cold.** This is when the person experiences really good times and then really bad times with a narcissist. In an effort to get things back to the really good times, they begin walking on eggshells, "turning themselves inside out" and trying to suppress and silence anything about themselves that will upset this other person. The reason the hot and cold cycle is so hard to escape, is that the target either feels compelled to stay because of all the good times, feels responsible for all the bad times, or feels that this time is different, that this time they finally got through to them, and that there will finally be no more lying, manipulating, cheating, siphoning funds, and so on. *The hot and cold cycle can also include the narcissist being "sweet and mean." Meaning, they may be very affectionate, attentive, and on their best behavior and then out of nowhere, a switch seems to flip where they become cold, cruel, and calloused in their treatment of the target.*

4. **Neglectful.** Neglectful behavior often goes hand-in-hand with other forms of abusive behavior. Neglectful behavior is when a person is taught to survive and be thankful for the physical or emotional crumbs that are given by the narcissist. Oftentimes if a person voices a complaint about the crumbs they are given, their concerns are minimized or dismissed, or spun around to accuse them of being ungrateful, selfish, or difficult.

The result of any of these types of abusive or neglectful patterns of behavior tend to leave a person feeling like they lack a solid sense of self, and confused as to what's "normal" and what's problematic as far as other people's behavior goes. This is because when a person has been continually told that what's problematic isn't a problem, or is somehow their fault, then they often find themselves living in a state of perpetual confusion. This can be likened to the story of "Alice in Wonderland," where nothing is like it seems and where they struggle with having a solid footing in what's really a problem and who has the problem.

This level of confusion and introspection is a large reason why people stay in abusive relationships for as long as they do, as well as why many people leave one abusive relationship only to find themselves in another one. (Because after an abusive relationship, the former target tends to doubt themselves and their perception of problematic behavior, which in turn makes them incredibly vulnerable—and odds are they don't even realize it.) I know this can sound terrifying, but please don't fret. I really think by the end of this book, everything will make a lot more sense.

In addition, it's very common for a person to start learning about narcissistic abuse and then to realize that there have been a lot of abusive people in their life over the years. And while this particular relationship might have been what made them realize there is a problem, they soon start to connect the dots and see that they've had a lot of narcissistic people in their life.

While this can feel overwhelming, it's all a part of your awakening and getting back into alignment with your authentic self. The beauty and power that can come from this awakening is that once you reconnect with your authentic self, you can then go about intentionally building an authentic life that you love, instead of settling for a life of mediocrity or unhappiness.

Chapter 4: Understanding Abuse

Abusive behavior is behavior that treats another person in a harsh or harmful way, and it falls into seven categories: verbal, emotional, psychological, sexual, financial, physical, and spiritual. Any of these types of abuse can be done in ways that are either overt (more outright or obvious) or covert (hidden or less outright or obvious).

Abusive behavior is driven by the need to gain and keep power and control over another person or situation. In order for an abusive person to have this mindset, they have to believe that they are *entitled and justified* to get and keep power and control over another. This is important because while their behavior might be causing their target pain, it's their mindset that's driving the problematic behavior. Even if this person stops being abusive in certain ways, odds are that the need to get and keep power and control would surface in other areas. For targets of abuse, this can feel like they are continually playing the game "whack a mole," where they try to address one problematic behavior only to later have another one surface. For example a narcissist may cheat, and then when their partner thinks the partner has stopped and that their relationship has turned a corner, they find out that they've been siphoning funds, or they start yelling, name calling or threatening, etc.

Abusive behavior isn't just limited to extreme physical abuse, and abusive behavior doesn't need to be ongoing over a long period of time in order for there to be major harm done. Abusive behavior also doesn't exist in a vacuum. If one form of abuse is present, then there are usually multiple forms present. The vast majority of the time (if not always) some form of verbal, emotional, psychological, sexual, financial, or spiritual abuse precedes physical abuse.

I think it's also vitally important to realize that while a person might not be directly physically abused, that doesn't somehow lessen the damage done by the other forms of abuse. Emotional, psychological, financial, sexual, verbal, or spiritual abuse is abuse—it can leave a person battered and bruised in ways that aren't visible, but that are just as serious and just as detrimental (if not more so), including causing PTSD, anxiety, depression, or leading a person to commit suicide. At the same time, physical abuse doesn't "just" leave physical bruises or scars, there is often deep psychological damage that is done.

Defining Abuse

Overt vs. Covert Abuse

Abusive behavior occurs in two main ways: overt and covert.

Overt abuse is any form of abuse that is outright or obvious. What is overt is largely dependent on a person's knowledge of what abuse is. For most people who are not familiar with abuse, overtly abusive behavior is that which someone can concretely point to and say, "This is abuse." The type of behavior that tends to fall into the overt category is usually extreme verbal abuse, such as yelling or name calling, sexual abuse, or physical abuse that leaves large, visible bruises or broken bones. However, if what a person is experiencing doesn't fit with their understanding of what abuse is, or with who can be abused—or who can be abusive, then what they are experiencing will most likely not register as abuse or even as problematic.

Example: Sarah had no problem calling her husband John all kinds of insulting names in front of their children or other people. Sarah's abuse was overt, as it was done in an outright manner. However, because Sarah never hit John or her children, along with the fact that she was female as well as a mother, John, his children, and other people didn't view her screaming, yelling, and name calling as abuse; they considered her to be "difficult" or "temperamental."

Example: Brian had been physically abusive towards Kate, leaving bruises on her face, neck, and arms. Brian's physical abuse was overt in that it was visible to both her and others.

Covert abuse is abuse that is generally considered to be hidden or less obvious. Covert abuse is done in a way that others, and often the person experiencing it, can't easily point to and say, "This is abuse." Covertly-abusive behavior tends to be verbal, emotional, psychological, sexual, financial, spiritual, and physical if it's done in a way that doesn't leave large bruises, broken bones, or otherwise is severe enough that others notice. Covert behavior is often much more insidious, and usually comes across as subtle put downs, biting sarcasm or cruel humor, intimidation, undermining, controlling, demeaning, and overall behavior that serves to disempower and diminish another person.

Covert abuse can be done in a wide variety of ways, including subtle digs about a person's education, income, gender, physical appearance, or age. It can be done by neglecting a person's needs, such as withholding affection, attention, or giving a person the silent treatment. Because covert abuse is less obvious than more overt forms of abuse, covert abuse is often seen as less hurtful or damaging than overt abuse; but it's not. It's just as damaging (if not more so) than overt abuse because covert abuse is a subtle and slow grinding down of another person. Often the target (and others—including many friends, family, and therapists) do not identify what is happening to them as abusive, or they minimize it, justifying the person's abusive behavior by chalking it up to "that's just how they are." They may blame the abusive person's childhood, the stress they are under, or problems with communication in the relationship. While these things may be occurring, that doesn't make abusing another person okay. When a person experiences covert abuse, they often feel "crazy" because they know something is off, and they start to feel ground down and drained by this other person. They often wonder if they are too sensitive, too emotional, or can't take a joke—either because they are continually told this by the abusive person or they are convincing themselves because they don't know why they feel this way.

It's also important to note that the vast majority of overt abuse begins with covert abuse. If a person is comfortable covertly or overtly abusing someone—especially in public—then odds are what they are doing behind closed doors is much worse.

However, once you are aware of all the different ways abusive behavior comes across, it won't be covert to you anymore. Not only will you see it for what it is, but you will most likely feel frustrated as hell by the sheer amount of people who don't see it as problematic, let alone abusive.

Example of covert psychological abuse: Ryan and Jane were dating, but that didn't stop Ryan from "making friends" with a bunch of women on Facebook. Ryan often hid his phone so that Jane wouldn't see the flirty messages he sent to these other women. He even slept with his phone under his pillow and would get upset if Jane even so much as touched it. Whenever Jane asked about his "squirrelly" behavior, Ryan accused her of being insecure, paranoid, crazy, jealous, and having major trust issues. He would flat out deny that he was hiding his phone and sending other women flirty messages, and he would tell Jane that she needed to see a therapist. Jane began to doubt her perception of events, and because Ryan was so adamant that he wasn't cheating, and that Jane was the one with issues, Jane began to doubt herself, and began to wonder if she really was insecure, jealous, and had trust issues. (Ryan's behavior is called "gaslighing.")

Example of covert verbal and emotional abuse: Sara's mother had teased and belittled her about her weight her whole life. If they were eating in public, her mother would "tease" her about what she was eating, call her names, or would make comments about her portions or food choices. Whenever Sara would tell her mother that her comments hurt her feelings, her mother would accuse her of being too sensitive, not able to take a joke, or not being able to handle the truth.

Example of covert verbal and emotional abuse: Peter and Kim were dating. Whenever Peter had a question or didn't know something that Kim did, she'd say something snarky like, "Well, that's why I went to college." If Peter mispronounced a word, Kim would take it as an opportunity to make fun of him and his "small town ignorance" as she called it. When Peter told her that he was upset by the way she treated him, she'd tell him that he was too sensitive and that she didn't mean anything bad by her comments—that she thought his stupidity was "cute" and that he needed to lighten up. Peter continually felt put down by Kim's comments, as though not only was he not as smart as Kim, but that he was too sensitive and didn't have a good sense of humor either.

Example of covert verbal abuse: Carla and Rachel were friends.

Whenever Rachel would do something that Carla didn't like, she'd pinch her. Even though Rachel told her to stop, Carla continued, saying that she was just playing and that Rachel needed to learn to take a joke. Rachel found herself constantly wondering if perhaps she was too sensitive.

Example of covert abuse (in general): Ken's mother, Phyllis, was a pillar of society, and everything she posted on Facebook showed that she was an amazing, charitable woman and a loving mother. Only those who really knew her realized that everything she did was all for show—and that behind closed doors she was incredibly physically, verbally, emotionally, and psychologically abusive to both Ken and his father. Phyllis' abuse was covert, as it was hidden from others, and she was charming to everyone outside of the home.

Misconceptions about Abuse

There are three strong social biases when it comes to abuse. Many people tend to think that abuse is only abuse if: a male is abusing a female; they are in a romantic relationship; the abuse is physical and frequent, resulting in a multitude of bruises or broken bones on a regular basis.

Outside of these three elements, abuse tends to be minimized, or in some situations, even glorified. I'm going to cover each point one at a time, as abuse can only exist when there is confusion about what it is. In addition, many people have been surrounded by abuse their whole lives and have struggled to pinpoint what exactly was wrong, because what they were experiencing didn't fall within those three elements.

Bias #1: Abuse is only abuse if a male is abusing a female.

Truth: Abuse is abuse, *regardless of the gender of the person doing it.* If the dynamic is flipped, and a female is abusing a male, the prevailing thought is that it is often that they must have done something wrong and deserved it…and if her abuse is towards a child, that the woman is being a good parent by going to such great lengths to discipline them. This is not only incorrect, it's dysfunctional and damaging thinking. Women can abuse men and other women, just like men can abuse women and other men.

Bias #2: Abuse is only abuse if two people are in a romantic relationship. Anything else is just "family dynamics" and needs to be resolved

Truth: Abuse is abuse, regardless of the dynamic between the two people. If a family member is abusive in any way, it's common for this to be seen as part of their family dynamics and the push is to "forgive and forget" and continue to allow this destructive person in their lives because they are family. Or if the abuse is anything outside of physical or sexual, it is often minimized and justified by enablers of the abusive person as them having a bad day, or a bad childhood, and that those on the receiving end of this abuse somehow need to be more "compassionate" and understanding of where they are coming from. This is incredibly revictimizing to those who are on the receiving end of abuse. All abuse is damaging, there is no excuse for it, and a person doesn't need to put up with it just because the abuser is family. Other dynamics that tend to fly under the radar are if the couple is same-sex, or not in a romantic relationship, but are "friends," neighbors, coworkers, or if the person is a spiritual leader, or works in a caring or trusted profession, such a police officer, teacher, or therapist.

Bias #3: Abuse is only abuse if it physical abuse and leaves a multitude of bruises, or puts someone in the hospital.

Truth: Physical abuse is just one type of abuse. There is also emotional, psychological, verbal, spiritual, financial, sexual, and spiritual abuse. All forms are incredibly damaging and can cause long-lasting effects, including PTSD and suicide.

Bias #4: Abuse only happens to adults.

Truth: Many children can and do experience abuse from either adults or from other children. Oftentimes children don't have a voice or an ability to get away from an abuser. It's important that we advocate for them. And it's important that we realize that "bullying" is abusive, and while it happens to many children, it isn't a normal part of growing up, and is highly problematic—and can lead to suicide.

Seven Types of Abusive Behavior

Emotional Abuse. Emotional abuse is any act that attempts to define, diminish, devalue, degrade, and/or demean another. Emotional abuse often goes along with verbal abuse, and damages a person's self-esteem and their self-worth.

Examples of emotional abuse include telling another person what they are thinking or feeling, calling them names, putting them down, hurting them with "brutal honesty," isolating them, using threats or intimidation to control them, undermining or attacking their self-esteem, chronic lying or cheating, giving the silent treatment, excessively criticizing, or blaming the target for the abuse.

Emotional abuse often results in a wide variety of emotional and physical disorders including (but not limited to) anxiety, nightmares, insomnia, dramatically decreased self-esteem, paranoia, insecurity, chronic depression, post-traumatic stress disorder (PTSD), and chronic pain.

Financial abuse is when one person damages or hinders another person's access to employment, money, or credit, with the ultimate goal of keeping power and control over their target. This might be done in order to prevent the target from having funds to leave the relationship, or it could be done because the narcissist is reckless and impulsive with money and buys whatever they want. Like others kinds of behavior, financial abuse can be overt or covert.

Examples of financial abuse would be the narcissist having secret accounts, spending all the money, driving the couple deep into debt, insisting on a joint account and then having complete control over it, grossly mismanaging funds, stealing money, siphoning money, damaging or destroying the target's credit, and opening up credit cards or taking out loans that the target doesn't know about but is responsible for. It can also be forbidding the target to work, insisting the target work and then insisting that they turn over all the money, manipulating the target out of their money by pretending to want to marry them, getting pregnant (or getting the target pregnant) intentionally in order to get child support or alimony.

Physical abuse is any form of intentional and unwanted contact that causes harm. This behavior can include pinching, slapping, punching, kicking, scratching, biting, hair pulling, pushing spanking, grabbing clothing, throwing objects at the target, forcing or coercing sex, holding the target down, strangling, or using a weapon on the target such as a gun, knife, mace, etc.

Psychological Abuse: Some mental-health professionals consider psychological and emotional abuse to be the same thing. However, many people (myself included) who have experienced both, consider emotional and psychological abuse to be different. The reason is that emotional abuse is about gaining power and control over another person's self-esteem whereas psychological abuse is about gaining power and control over a person's perception of reality. Psychological abuse erodes a person's reality and replaces it with that of their abuser, whereas emotional abuse erodes a person's sense of self-worth and self-esteem.

Some examples of psychological abuse would be telling a person they are something that they are not, telling a person events happened a certain way when they did not, moving objects around and denying that they've been moved, or that the target is "crazy" or losing their mind.

Example: Scott and Diana lived several hours away from each other. They made plans for Scott to drive up to Diana's place so they could spend the weekend together. On Thursday, Scott told Diana how excited he was to go to an art festival with her that weekend in his hometown. Diana was confused, and told him that she didn't know anything about an art show. She thought he was coming to visit her. Scott gently teased her saying that she must be confused. The plan was for her to visit him, and to go to the art festival. Diana felt like her head was spinning. She vividly remembered them planning for him to come to her house. She assumed she must have misremembered, because even though she's sure that that wasn't their plan, she can't think of a good reason as to why Scott would lie about something like that.

Example: Helen is in the middle of a divorce from her husband, Ben, due to his chronic cheating and lying. Ben continues to harass and psychologically push Helen over the edge, telling her that she's worthless, no one will ever want her, and that she should kill herself. Helen is so emotionally distraught, that she is finding herself wondering if perhaps Ben is right and that she should end her life.

Example: Beth and Trey had been married for six months when her good friend told her Trey was on several dating sites and texted her some screen shots of his dating profile. Beth was devastated. She thought they were happily married and was shocked to find out that he was cheating. Trey became really angry and denied it. When Beth showed him the screen shot her friend had sent, he said that wasn't him and both her and her friend were crazy. He accused her of looking for a reason to break up with him because that online dating profile was just some guy that looked like him. He told her that he couldn't handle much more of her jealousy and insecurity, and that she needed therapy—and that if she ever pulled something like this again that he'd leave. Beth was confused, and began to doubt herself and her friend. She began to cry and apologize profusely.

Sexual abuse is any sort of sexual contact where consent was either not given, or not given freely due to real or perceived pressure, fear, or intimidation, or if the target was not of sound mind, legal age, or was under the influence of drugs or alcohol.

Sexual abuse can and does happen to men, women, and children of any age and isn't limited to molestation or rape. It can also include refusal to use contraception, using sex toys or other objects on a person without their consent, intentionally getting pregnant or getting someone pregnant without the other partner's consent, deliberately causing unwanted physical pain or humiliation during sex, as well as deliberately passing on sexually transmitted diseases.

Example: Tina and Tom met at a party and had been drinking. Tom found his way into the guest bedroom and passed out. He woke up to find Tina trying to have sex with him. He tried to protest, and she became offended, suggesting that he must be gay. Tom could tell by how upset she was that she would probably spread such a rumor around school. He decided to have sex with her out of fear she would start a rumor or try to destroy his reputation. Tom felt violated, but like many men, didn't identify that he was sexually abused/assaulted because he didn't realize that a guy could be sexually assaulted by a female.

Example: Tony was having an affair on his wife with Kendra, his coworker. Kendra became involved with Tony because he told her his marriage was over, and that his wife was controlling and manipulative. The truth was that Tony had no intention of leaving his wife; he just wanted to have sex with Kendra. Kendra kept asking him when he would file divorce papers, and Tony gave her the silent treatment for two weeks. When he returned, he told her that he needed time to sort out his feelings, and he officially ended things with Kendra. However, he wanted to keep Kendra around, so he continued to call and spend time with her. He intentionally got Kendra pregnant by poking holes in his condoms and pretended to be shocked when he learned of her pregnancy. He reassured Kendra that he would be there for her and their child.

Example: Roger and Sandra are married, and shortly after their honeymoon Roger told Sandra that he expects her to have sex with him anytime he wants it, because that is her job as his wife—and that if she didn't, he would have sex with other women.

Spiritual abuse is gaining power and control over a person through the use of their spiritual or religious belief system. This is generally done by using the threat of God's wrath, or by manipulating a person by claiming that their abusive demands are God's will or somehow a part of what it means to be spiritual person. Spiritual abuse can also occur with multiple members of a congregation who may be pushing a person to stay in an abusive relationship because it is deemed by them to be their spiritual obligation, or is somehow the moral thing to do.

Example: Travis' mother was physically, verbally, and emotionally abusive. She was also a devout Catholic. Travis had tried to cut off contact with his mother for years, but each time he started to distance himself from her, his mother would tell him that the Bible said that he needed to honor his mother, and that he would have to answer to God for his mistreatment of her.

Example: Sam and Maria had been married for fifteen years. During that time, they were both active members of their church, and Sam was even looked to by some to be a "prophet." He held Bible studies at their house on a regular basis, and everyone at church seemed to really like him. However, when they were alone, Sam continually abused Maria by yelling, calling her names, and raping her. Whenever she would cry or try to protest, Sam would tell her that if she was a good Christian that she would submit to him, and to stop making him feel like he was raping her because a husband couldn't rape his wife. Maria had thought about leaving for close to ten years, but she stayed because Sam would continually cite Biblical scripture to her and tell her that God hates divorce and that if she would just submit to what Sam wanted, they wouldn't have problems with their marriage.

Verbal Abuse is abuse that surrounds using (or not using) spoken language in order to get and keep power and control over someone. Verbal abusers tend to attack and slowly and systematically grind down their target's individuality and sense of self. Like most abuse, verbal abuse (especially more covert forms) tend to be done in a way that's presented as no big deal, or as though what they are saying is the truth, which eventually grooms their target to accept hurtful or harmful behavior.

Some examples of verbal abuse are: blaming, shaming, "brutal honesty," denying events, name calling, yelling, threatening, undermining, patronizing, making hurtful jokes or sarcasm, minimizing, blocking, diverting, criticizing, making false promises, and having angry outbursts. Verbal abuse can also be nonverbal, such as withholding important information, stonewalling, or giving someone the silent treatment.

Verbal abuse often leaves a person feeling like they are walking on eggshells, can't do anything right, anxious, insecure, uncertain, doubting of their own perception of events, reality, or their own sanity.

Example: Tina and Roger were dating, and the fact that he didn't go to college (whereas Tina has a PhD in education), and instead opted to start his own landscaping company seemed to be something that Tina focused on, and jabbed him about… relentlessly. Whenever Roger pronounced a word wrong, or misspelled something, Tina made sure to point it out, and would make snarky comments such as, "That's so cute that you said that word wrong…your ignorance is so entertaining." Roger brushed this off the first few times, but he's no longer finds it funny, and he's noticed that he feels as if he's continually walking on eggshells, and even second guessing his abilities at work. The last comment Tina made was, "It's amazing people even hire you with how misspelled your invoices are. They must hire you because you are so likable, because we both know that it's not because of how professional you are." When Roger told her that he didn't appreciate being talked to like that, Tina told him that she was just being honest, that he was too sensitive, and she was just trying to help.

Example: Even though Amanda was thirty years old, her mother would fly into a rage whenever Amanda tried to set a boundary with her or disagreed with her. Her mother would tell Amanda that she was difficult, ungrateful, spoiled, stupid, or worthless. It took Amanda years to realize that what her mother was saying was abusive and not true.

How to Recognize an Abusive Relationship

An abusive relationship is any dynamic between two people in which abuse is present. I use the word "dynamic" because it's important to realize that abusive behavior isn't limited to married couples or people in a romantic relationship. An abusive dynamic can exist between a parent and a child, a brother and a sister, between two "friends," between two coworkers, and so on.

However, just like those who are in a cult do not realize that they are in a cult, most people in an abusive relationship do not realize that they are in an abusive relationship. To them, what they are experiencing has become normal—especially if they grew up in something similar or worse. They may realize that the abusive person has a lot of "problematic" behavior, and that their relationship has problems, but oftentimes feel at least partially responsible for how they are treated. They may feel like a failure for wanting to leave (especially if doing so is against their religion). They may feel stuck because they have children with this person, or because they don't have the financial means to leave. They may feel confused, crazy, ground down, incapable, anxious, depressed, or suicidal. They may think that if they can just get through to their partner about the problematic behavior, their partner will change, and they will often hold on to the relationship until things become so outrageously problematic that they are forced to leave.

The analogy of how to boil a frog is often used to describe how people get (and stay) in abusive relationships. In order to boil a frog, you can't throw it in boiling water, because it will jump out. You have to place it in lukewarm water and then slowly turn the heat up. The frog doesn't realize what is happening, but once it realizes it is in danger, the situation has become really extreme and dangerous.

The "lukewarm water" of abusive relationships tends to happen in five main ways: hot and cold, sweet and mean, cold and cruel, good and bad, or some sort of hybrid of these four.

Hot and Cold relationships start with the target being showered with excessive amounts of attention and/or affection (love bombing) which leaves them feeling like they've met their soul mate. Then, out of the blue, the attention and affection dries up to a trickle or stops altogether. This leaves the target in a frantic scramble to renew the affection and attention from their partner. When their partner runs cold, targets often feel as though they somehow pushed away their soul mate, and intense depression, introspection, and rehashing of events and what they could have done different often follows.

Sweet and Mean relationships tend to start with an abusive person who, at first, seems kind, considerate, compassionate, charming, and intense. When their mask starts to slip, they become cruel and abusive. This is also commonly referred to as a "Dr. Jekyll and Mr. Hyde" character, and oftentimes this erratic behavior leaves the target confused by what they are experiencing. This leads the victim to walk more and more on eggshells in an attempt to keep the "Mr. Hyde" side of their partner from surfacing.

Cold and Cruel is a relationship where the abusive person gives their target "crumbs" of attention or affection, then becomes cruel and abusive or cold, calloused, and indifferent, leaving the target to feel perpetually starved out emotionally and physically.

Good and Bad is when things may be going fine or even wonderful between two people…until the target discovers their partner has been living a double life. This dynamic leaves the target feeling like they are on an emotional roller coaster, as the good times are really good, but the bad times are really bad, and they wonder if this relationship is a fairy tale or a total nightmare.

None of these four patterns of behavior are found in healthy relationships.

- How Being in an Abusive Relationship Feels

- An abusive relationship is a confusing and crazy-making relationship. Here are some common ways people feel during and after an abusive relationship:

- Feeling perpetually confused and wondering if what you are experiencing is really problematic or if you are making a big deal out of it.

- Embarrassed or humiliated when your partner treats you "like this" (abusively) in front of others.

- Ashamed that you are being treated this way.

- Needing to walk on eggshells and avoiding certain topics because of how this person will react.

- Feeling responsible for their abusive treatment—like it's somehow your fault, especially if you are being blamed for their behavior. (If you hadn't forgotten to buy milk, they wouldn't have yelled at you.)

- Thinking that you need to work harder at communicating better (or not bringing up certain topics) so they don't become abusive again.

- Feeling like you can't say no or disagree without consequences such as a fight, silent treatment, or getting attacked either verbally and/or physically.

- Feeling like you can't (or don't want to) tell others the full truth about your partner's behavior, because they'd be horrified by how you are being treated.

- Feeling defensive whenever anyone points out that your partner is a "jerk" or is abusive.

- Feeling distrusting, anxious, fearful, confused, and depressed around others (as well as the abusive person).

- Fearful of their yelling, cussing, hitting, breaking up with you out of the blue, or giving the silent treatment again.

- Overwhelmed or fearful of leaving, and what that person might do.

- Apologizing for them, or justifying what happened (they were tired/hungry/abused as a child/spoiled as a child, etc.)

- Fearful that this person might hurt you or your children.

- Googling their behavior in an attempt to figure out what's going on.

None of these elements or feelings are present in a healthy relationship.

Chapter 5: Terms and Definitions

In the next chapter are some of the more common words and concepts that a person will come across in a support group for narcissistic abuse.

Before I get into the terms and definitions, I want to bring up some pros and cons that people often have with the terms. Many of these terms can clarify what a person has experienced—which is really helpful if they've been fumbling around in the dark trying to understand what is going on. When a person learns that there are terms that describe what they went through, it is incredibly validating in and of itself. The downside of terms and definitions is that people can feel mean, judgmental, or harsh with using them.

When people first come across these terms or concepts, one of four main things tends to happen:

    1. They aren't comfortable using the term.

    2. They want to make sure the term is 100% accurate.

    3. Everything makes sense, and they insist on using

the term (oftentimes much to the annoyance of their friends, family—and even some therapists).

4. Everything makes sense, and while the term is helpful, they view it more as a pointer to the behavior.

Let me address these four points one at a time and explain them a little more.

1. They aren't comfortable using the term. Most people in general aren't comfortable using labels that shine a light onto problematic behavior—whether that behavior is their own or someone else's. This is especially the case with the topic of abuse, and especially if a person has hope that this other person can change. For a person to fully realize that their mother or spouse is abusive can be a harsh reality to handle, and it can take a while for a person to come to terms what they are experiencing is, in fact, abusive.

They might tell themselves something like, "Well, my mother is really 'difficult,' yes, she screams, yells, and continually belittles me whenever I do something she doesn't like, but she never hits me, so I'm not really comfortable with saying she's abusive."

For these reasons, it's very common for a person to minimize what they are experiencing, and some people never get to the place where they are comfortable using certain terms to describe their experience. (This is often the situation within families, where one sibling—usually the one who was the target of abuse—realizes that a family member is abusive, while the other siblings or family members continue to minimize, deny, or justify the abusive person's behavior because they are family.)

2. They want to make sure the label is 100% accurate.
Wanting clarity about a label's accuracy, especially when it comes to personality disorders, makes total sense. However, ask any mental health professional, and they'll tell you that diagnosing personality disorders isn't an exact science, nor is it something that is cut and dried. Personality "disorders" are traits that exist on a spectrum ranging from mild to severe which negatively impact the lives of those around them, as well as their own life—even if the person doesn't realize that they have a problem.

One reason for this needing clarity may be that the person doing the research has heard from their therapist or support groups that those with Narcissistic Personality Disorder or Antisocial Personality Disorder do not change, and that therapy doesn't help (and oftentimes it makes their behavior worse—as they often will use the information they gather in therapy to better manipulate others). So, they want to make absolutely sure that this other person really has an issue that won't change before they leave the relationship or dynamic. They may fear giving up too soon with trying to fix the relationship, or trying to help this person, thinking that if they can just get through to them, or get them enough therapy, rehab, religion, or love, that they could become a good partner. They don't want to walk away from someone they have built a life with, someone they also feel an intense, deep, soul-mate type connection with (which is a very common feeling if you are in a friendship or intimate relationship with an emotional manipulator of any kind).

I know that a lot of validation can come with a diagnosis; however, it's vitally important to realize that problematic behavior of any degree is still problematic, and it's up to you to figure out what your deal breakers are. I think the big take away with the concept of personality disorders isn't in getting a diagnosis, it is in realizing that some people out there have personalities that are really problematic, and that these people do not have the same morals or values that you do. And more importantly, these people lack empathy and remorse, meaning, they do not have a conscience, and that they never will.

3. Everything makes sense, and they insist on using these labels. People often come across a term and suddenly everything makes sense. All the confusion is lifted, and they start to see problematic behavior a lot more clearly. Because they now have clarity after being in a fog of confusion for so long, they often feel that their new understanding has been hard-won, and that these labels help to validate their experience, and they get really upset when others imply they are just using certain terms (especially narcissist, sociopath, or abuse) because they are bitter and jaded, or that they are making too big of a deal out of things.

4. Everything makes sense, and while the term is helpful, they view it more as a pointer to the behavior. These people also experience a lot of clarity when coming across the different terms and concepts, and most likely also feel revicitimized by friends, family, and therapists who minimize or discount their experience, or who try to discourage them from using the labels. These people most likely have gotten to the place where they are tired of fighting an uphill battle to justify and defend their experiences with people having abusive behavior—especially with those who have never experienced anything like it—and so they bypass the argument and instead view the terms as "pointers" to validation, concepts, and the resulting clarity.

I have had each of these four mindsets at different points in my life too, and had I written this book a few years ago, I would have fought hard for people to use terms like narcissist and sociopath, because I did feel that those realizations were hard-won, and I really wanted people to acknowledge what I went through was real, and outside the realm of "normal" bad behavior or a "bad breakup." I still find it mind boggling, infuriating, minimizing, and dangerous that there are so many people with outrageously abusive and exploitative behavior walking this Earth, and that the vast majority of society (including many therapists) don't see it for what it is.

I've since learned that the best outlet for my frustration, time, and sanity is spent focused on my healing, as well as empowering others to reclaim their power and control and to move forward in their own understanding and healing. In short, those who are ready to acknowledge what abusive behavior is will acknowledge it, and those that won't, won't.

So here's my advice on how to move forward with these terms: Hold onto what helps; let the rest go.

If you find yourself getting hung up on the different terms, it helps to look at them as pointers. Because while these words can give tremendous clarity, the behaviors and concepts that the terms point to are really what's most important. Problematic behavior is problematic behavior, regardless of the term assigned to it.

Definitions

Abuse by proxy: This is when a narcissist either recruits other people into abusing their target for them (also referred to as a "flying monkey"), or abuses their target through other people. The people recruited to abuse the target have generally been manipulated by the narcissist into thinking that the narcissist is the victim. Those who have been sucked into this manipulation may or may not even know the target. If they know the target, they may be the target's own friends, family, co-workers, people at church, or even children. If they don't know the target, then they are most likely the narcissist's newest target. Oftentimes these people are good people who think they are doing the right thing by shaming, blaming, or harassing the target, but this is because the narcissist has twisted the facts and has conveniently left out everything that they did to the target.

When an abusive person continues to abuse their target through another person, this may be ongoing (which is often the case with flying monkeys), or it can be done by getting another person to say or do something that serves to undermine, provoke, take jabs at their target's self-esteem, or instill fear or intimidation.

Example: Teri was verbally and emotionally abusive to her girlfriend Jane. Jane thought that given enough time, love, and therapy that Teri could change—which she didn't. The final straw for Jane was when she found out that Teri had been cheating on her. A few weeks after their breakup, Jane started to get dirty looks from people, and found out that Teri has told a bunch of lies about her, saying that she cheated on her, and that she was abusive, jealous, controlling, and possessive. Teri is shocked that Jane would lie like this, and is even more shocked when she starts getting nasty messages (calling her names) from people she doesn't know on Facebook.

Example: Greg and Paula had been married for ten years before

Paula fully realized she was in an abusive marriage. Each time Greg would become abusive, he would bring her flowers or apologize the next day. Things would be fine for a few weeks, but then he'd start up again. She finally had enough when their ten year-old son, Brian, began calling her names and treating her with the same disdain and contempt that Greg did. Greg's behavior escalated after their divorce, and he began making all kinds of threats, such as he wasn't going to pay child support, and how Paula ruined his life and that she was going to pay for this. Paula ended up getting a restraining order against Greg. About two week later, her neighbor came by with a bouquet of flowers for her that had been delivered to his address that had her name on them, but didn't say who the sender was. Paula felt a wave of fear wash over her, as she knew these flowers were from Greg, as these were the kind he normally sent. She also knew that these flowers weren't being sent as an apology; they were being sent so she'd get the message that he still had ways of contacting her if he wanted to, and that he wasn't going to let a restraining order stop him. (Greg was continuing to abuse Paula through her neighbor—even though the neighbor didn't realize he was participating in anything other than delivering flowers.)

Anticipation: Anticipation is the number-one tool targets have in their defense against abuse. By anticipating what kind of actions they think the abuser will take, the target shifts from being reactive to being responsive. Being reactive means that the abuser acts, then the target reacts, and because the target is in reaction mode, they lose what limited control they did have over the situation. Being responsive means the target anticipates that the narcissist will try and knock them off balance emotionally in order to provoke a reaction.

Anticipating how to respond to a person who continually tries to knock you off balance by provoking you, or who has erratic and intimidating behavior starts with emotionally detaching as much as you can from the situation and from the person, and seeing their behavior for what it is: abusive. Once you realize they are trying to get you upset, or that they are trying to intimidate you, or that they are dangerous, and that they are not a friend, a parent, or a soul mate, then you can start to take appropriate action to keep yourself safe. Once you realize what's going on, it's a lot easier (although it still takes practice) to slow things down enough to stay grounded in your planned response.

Example: Kyla and Lionel were married. Lionel had no shortage of vindictive and hateful behavior. Kyla got to the point where she wanted a divorce but was scared of how Lionel would react. She decided to try and develop a plan and to anticipate his reactions to her leaving, based on how he'd reacted to her trying to leave before. This way, she could prepare herself as much as possible ahead of time for anything he might do. She also decided that since she could only anticipate his behavior to a certain extent, she'd be best off erring on the side of caution when it came to making decisions involving any potential interaction with Lionel.

Example: Jenny and Paul were recently divorced and had a daughter, Haley. Even though it was in their divorce decree that Jenny was to pick up Haley every Wednesday at five pm and have her home by nine pm, with Haley having done her homework and having already had dinner, it never failed that Jenny would bring her home late, generally with Haley not having eaten or her homework done. This would lead to long nights for both Haley and Paul, as he'd have to stay up and make sure homework was done and that Haley would get dinner. Paul began to anticipate Jenny's behavior and changed his routine with Haley so that she would have her homework done dinner eaten before she went out with Jenny. When Jenny found out about this, she was enraged, but because Paul anticipated this, he explained that this was easier for Haley and gave them more time together. Since this explanation made it seem like Paul was doing this for Jenny, she became less hostile towards him.

Antisocial Personality Disorder: The terms "sociopath" and "psychopath" were at one time considered two different personality disorders in the DSM (Diagnostic and Statistical Manual of Mental Disorders), however, over time these have been combined under the term "Antisocial Personality Disorder" (ASPD). Outside of a clinical setting, most people still refer to those with ASPD as sociopaths or psychopaths.

Some common traits of ASPD are that the person is usually charming, highly manipulative (using domination, charm, guilt, sympathy, pity, obligation, or intimidation to get their way), has a disregard for rules and others (usually behaviors that are based in either exploitation or cruelty often leading to time in jail as an adult), has a lack of remorse, and a lack of empathy (although they can do an award-winning performance to really make others believe that they are sorry and that this time will be different).

Example: Jill met John shortly after she graduated from college. It was a whirlwind relationship, and Jill remembers how she instantly felt a soul-mate connection with John. He was charming, funny, and intelligent and pursued her relentlessly. When they became engaged, John's mother pulled her aside and tried to warn her about him. She said, "There is something wrong with John. He lacks the ability to love." Jill always thought that was an odd thing for a mother to say about her own son. Jill married him anyhow, and their relationship was a series of over-the-top amazing behavior followed by the discovery of jaw-dropping awful behavior that she never saw coming, such as chronic cheating, lying, credit cards she didn't know about, and an overall total lack of regard for how his actions impacted her or anyone else. It was like John was a great guy until she found out he wasn't. Then, he'd flip a switch and go back to being this amazing guy that everyone loved.

Jill often said that John lied so much, that he'd lie even if the truth would work better for him. Jill believed in commitment and marriage and didn't want to divorce John…and John was relying on that, so he'd continue to say or do enough of the right things (or would prey upon Jill's good nature, using guilt and sympathy) to get her to stay. It wasn't until Jill's mother encouraged her to join a support group for narcissistic abuse that she realized she wasn't in a marriage, she was trapped in a manipulation, and if John really loved her he wouldn't be cheating, lying, and siphoning funds out of their account to take other women on dates.

Example: Sarah was incredibly charming and had most people around her thinking she was a devoted wife and mother. She ran a successful real-estate firm and led a women's group at her church every Sunday. Only her family and very few people knew that she was a pathological liar, cheater, and incredibly selfish. Her husband has had to run off more than one of her boyfriends, but he always took her back because she seemed so sincere when she promised this would never happen again. Sarah's children grew to resent her for all of her lies and emp-ty promises. Her youngest daughter recently told her father that she felt Sarah just wanted to have kids because they were like props to make her look good, and Sarah's husband often wondered the same. He couldn't understand how a woman could be so emotionally detached from her children, but when other people were around she could act like mother of the year. Sarah's husband recently found out that she embezzled over $150,000 from the escrow funds in her real estate account. When he confronted her about this, she began fake crying and blamed her stealing on voices she was hearing, and her cheat-ing on being a sex addict. Her husband was shocked by this, as she'd never mentioned hearing voices before, or a sex addiction, and his anger at her softened into concern and was redirected into getting Sarah the help she needed…which is exactly what Sarah wanted.

Example: Susan met Rick on the internet. She knew about him from around town. He had several children by several different women and a history of jail time for theft and domestic violence. But despite all this, she found herself really drawn to him. He gave her more attention than any man ever had, and for the first time in her life, she felt like she really mattered. When Susan asked about his previous relationships, Rick told her that all of his exes were either addicts, bipolar, or had cheated on him, and that they had filed false charges against him which kept him from seeing his children. Susan felt bad for him, as he seemed like such a great guy who had run into many problematic women. She believed everything he told her, and within a few months they were married. Soon into their relationship, she became pregnant, and that's when Rick began to verbally and physically abuse her.

Several months later she found out that she had an STD, and when she confronted Rick about it, he flew into a rage and began accusing her of cheating on him, which she hadn't. During their fight, Susan went into premature labor. Rick became even more upset when she called 911 to go to the hospital, and told her that she was just being dramatic and manipulative and trying to get him into trouble with the law. Rick refused to go to the hospital with her, and Susan delivered the baby later that night. Susan texted him to let him know she had a boy. Much to her surprise and sadness, he never bothered to text back. The social worker at the hospital encouraged her to go to a domestic violence shelter, and Susan was shocked when she mentioned this. She knew her relationship with Rick wasn't the best, but she didn't think it was abusive. She went to the shelter, and when she filed for divorce, Rick became threatening, and began telling everyone around town that the baby wasn't his, and that she was a gold digger who was trying to trap him into paying child support. To make matters worse, his friends and family believed him, and Susan was being stalked and harassed everywhere she went. She ended up contacting two of his exes, who told her that their experience with Rick was the same—that he started out as this amazing man, but over time became a total nightmare, and for Susan to run and never look back.

Apology: A sincere apology only exists when there are three elements present: 1. Someone sincerely and fully acknowledges what they've done wrong, 2. It doesn't happen again, and 3. Massive action is taken to repair the damage done to the relationship.

If any of these three elements aren't present, then it's not a sincere apology.

If a narcissist blames you or anyone (or anything) for their abusive behavior, they aren't owning it—and if they aren't owning their behavior, they aren't going to be motivated to change it, because in their mind it's not their fault. In addition, even if a narcissist does actually apologize, but their behavior doesn't change for long (or it took years before it surfaced again)—then they aren't truly sorry. Another way to tell if they are truly sorry is if they are willing to take massive action to repair the damage done to the relationship. This is especially the case if they are cheating. If a person cheats, they need to be willing to answer any questions that their partner might have, as well as realize that it's going to take years to build up some degree of trust again. What happens with most narcissists is that they get caught for some sort of bad behavior, they deny it until they can't deny it anymore, and then they start blaming everyone else for what they did. Getting to the truth is like pulling teeth, and what's even more exhausting and crazy-making, is that they'll often insist that their target needs to trust them, and if the target doesn't, then they'll claim that the target is living in the past or is insecure! For the record, it's normal, healthy, and reasonable to have trust issues with a person who has lying issues. In addition, old issues aren't brought up…only unresolved ones are—and they are generally unresolved because the target still has questions or their partner still has squirrelly behavior.

Example of an apology: I'm sorry that I got upset and yelled at you. It wasn't okay that I reacted that way, and it won't happen again.

Examples of some typical "apologies" from narcissists:

- I'm sorry you feel that way.

- I told you I wouldn't cheat on you again. Damn. Quit bringing up the past.

- It's not my fault you can't take a joke.

- You were the best thing that's ever happened to me. I think we should go to therapy. How can you give up on us so easily?

- I'm sorry for what I did, but you aren't perfect either.

BDSM: Is an overlapping acronym that stands for **B**ondage and **D**iscipline, **D**omination and **S**ubmission, **S**adism and **M**asochism. BDSM can either be a lifestyle or have some elements of erotic play that are introduced from time-to-time to spice things up in the bedroom. The core of BDSM is that it is based around the safe, sane, and consensual explorations of power and control in a dynamic between the people involved.

The reason I bring this term up is because with the popularity of the book and movie, "Fifty Shades of Grey" lots of people have become interested in BDSM. I think it's important to separate out elements of abusive relationships from one where someone is wanting to be either dominant or submissive, because if that line isn't clear, then a person can be in what they think is a BDSM relationship when really it's abusive.

For starters, the underlying relationship before any BDSM elements are brought in, needs to be based on consent and respect. If those two elements aren't there, then the relationship is abusive, and will only become more abusive when BDSM gets added to the mix.

The dynamic between Anastasia and Christian in "Fifty Shades of Gray" is abusive, and it involves BDSM. It is not abusive because of the BDSM; it's abusive because he has no respect for her boundaries, his attraction to her is based purely on her innocence and how he can groom her into his ideal partner. He stalks her, makes major life decisions for her, manipulates her, steamrolls over her boundaries, and she never knows where she stands with him.

Some of the major differences between BDSM and abuse are:

In a BDSM dynamic there is an agreed exchange and exploration of power and control between two consenting adults.

In an abusive dynamic there is no agreed upon exchange—the dominating partner takes power and control away from the other person.

In a BDSM dynamic safe words are generally used (and considered a good idea to prevent unwanted boundary violations).

In an abusive dynamic there is no safe word or words that stop the abuse.

In a BDSM dynamic the submissive partner is the one with all the power, as they have a safe word and their boundaries are respected. Nothing happens to them that they haven't agreed to.

In an abusive dynamic the domineering partner is the one with all the power.

In a BDSM dynamic the exchange of power and control hinges on what is consensual—and nothing happens to the submissive partner that they are not okay with.

In an abusive dynamic none of the behavior is consensual. The other person is being used, abused, and exploited for the narcissist's personal satisfaction or gain.

Baiting: Much like how a fisherman puts bait on the end of a hook in order to catch a fish, a narcissist will put a provocative statement on their "hook" in order to catch their target. Narcissists typically bait their targets with angering and upsetting statements (usually subtle or not-so subtle put downs, or accusing the target of their behavior). These statements are designed to elicit a strong emotional response (usually anger or jealousy) from their target, usually with the intent to agitate and irritate their target to where they explode—and when they do the narcissist feels like they've "won." Many narcissists will do or say things to provoke an emotion (bait their target) in order for them to feel justified in their abuse. Once their target shows a reaction, the narcissist will either deny it or act surprised by their target's reaction, then spin the conversation around to where their target's reaction is the focus (and problem).

So while the target is busy trying to explain themselves, defend their feelings, and gain clarity about why communication got so far off track so fast—the narcissist is busy feeling self-satisfied by provoking their target into working so hard to defend themselves, watching them unravel, or trying to resolve the fight (which the narcissist keeps switching issues, so the fight can never be resolved). It's one of the many manipulative and sadistic games a narcissist plays in order to keep power and control over their target.

The narcissist will either stay cool, calm, and collected and act as though they have no idea as to why the target is so upset, or they will become more upset than the target and exclaim that they can't handle the target's jealousy, insecurity, issues, hyper-sensitivity, craziness/delusional/bipolar/problematic behavior, and declare that the target needs therapy or medication. In addition, the narcissist will often accuse their target of saying or doing the very thing that they are, such as wanting to fight, which can an added layer of crazy-making, and leave the target questioning their reality.

A technique that has worked well for me when dealing with narcissists has been to ask myself, "What emotion do I feel they are trying to provoke right now (or have a pattern of provoking)…and why?" and then following that up with, "How can I anticipate this and respond instead?" It is really hard not to engage when you are being poked like this, but it is possible. It really does help to realize that they are doing this intentionally, and their goal is to get a reaction. Once you see it for what it is, it's a lot easier to avoid getting hooked. Make it easy on yourself and block as many of their communication attempts as possible.

Example: Dawn finally decided to go "no contact" with her friend Gary. She'd known something was off for a while. Most of their conversations left her feeling angry, defensive, and irritated, but she couldn't quite pinpoint why. She enjoyed spending time with Gary as he was interesting, intelligent, and funny, but she felt like he always made little jabs at her, or the conversation would go off track, and she would end up on the defensive. She couldn't figure out why this always seemed to happen. To confuse matters more, when she brought up her concerns with Gary, he didn't seem to know what she was talking about. In their last conversation, Gary asked her opinion about some furniture he was thinking about buying, as Laura staged homes for a living. While she was telling him her opinion, he stopped her and said, "Oh never mind, I'll ask Gina. She's an interior designer and she'll know best. After all, she's a real professional." When Laura got upset, Gary seemed surprised by her reaction. Laura couldn't tell if she was being too sensitive or if Gary was just clueless. Finally, she decided that it didn't matter if it was her or Gary. She realized that didn't feel these subtle jabs by anyone else in her life, and she was tired of continually feeling like Gary was trying to insult her.

Here are some examples of phrases that a narcissist might use to bait their target:

- "You are being really immature." (When the target breaks up with the narcissist and goes "no contact" after being cheated on, threatened, or yelled at by them.)

- "I am so happy now that I don't have to deal with your craziness anymore." (Usually a text sent to evoke anger, hurt feelings, or even with the intent to push their target to suicide. These kinds of messages are usually sent shortly after the relationship has ended.)

- "I hate you; you ruined my life." (A message usually sent to evoke anger or confusion when the target has finally broken up with them after this last abusive episode, and the target is usually feeling like the abusive person is the one who ruined their life—not the other way around.)

- "How can you give up on us so easily?" (A message designed to shift the blame to their target, after the target has put up with lying, cheating, stealing—none of which has been easy to put up with, and leaving the narcissist is the hardest thing they've ever had to do.)

- "You are the manipulative and abusive one." (A message designed to shift the blame from themselves to their target, as well as to evoke anger in the target.)

Borderline Personality Disorder (BPD): A personality disorder that usually includes impulsive and risky behavior, unstable and intense relationships, highly manipulative behavior, frequent outbursts of anger/poor emotional regulation, unstable or fragile self-image, and suicidal behavior or threats of self-harm. There is a lot of overlap between Narcissistic Personality Disorder, Antisocial Personality Disorder, and Borderline Personality Disorder.

However, it's also important to know that many trauma specialists believe that PTSD is often misdiagnosed as Borderline Personality Disorder. It's very common for a person to get out of an abusive relationship and feel "unstable" (psychologically abused), "have a poor self-image" (because they've been ground down), "impulsive and risky behavior" (because they struggle with what's normal behavior after living with a crazy maker), "poor emotional control" (because they've been traumatized), and "feel suicidal" (because they are emotionally devastated and generally have PTSD).

Many targets of narcissists tend to be diagnosed with BPD, which can be devastating, as then they wonder if the narcissist was right—that they were the problem all along. Please know that even if you do have BPD or have some sort of mental illness such as bipolar, it is still no excuse for being abused.

Borderline Personality Disorder is often treated with a therapy called Dialectal Behavioral Therapy (DBT) which helps a person understand and express their feelings. (Frankly, DBT is something I wish could be taught starting with children in kindergarten, as we all could benefit from it.)

Boundaries: I like to think of boundaries as the body guard of our standards. Boundaries are the limits that we set (or don't set) for our standards of how we expect to be treated. These expectations are often subconscious and are instilled in us at an early age.

Unfortunately, having healthy boundaries is something that is not taught, let alone role-modeled to most children (or adults).

In fact, most people grow up learning unhealthy boundaries and standards from a wide variety of sources which might include their parents, friends, religion, community, gender role models, cultural expectations, music, movies, media, and so on. It can (and usually does) take a person several decades before they realize that their boundaries need work because we are all our own baseline for normal. Most of us have been this way our whole lives, so we might not have noticed that there was an issue. We might have noticed we had a pattern of problematic people or one-sided relationships and/or friendships in our life, or that we were continually giving to the point where we were worn out, but for many people, we don't see the pattern and tend to think that these problematic people or situations were isolated events.

This does not mean that being in an abusive relationship is your fault. It's not. Emotional manipulators are masters at eroding people's boundaries—especially if we continually rationalize when someone is pushing our boundaries. Because these boundary erosions are slow and steady, targets are often manipulated for years or decades before they realize what's happening. And again, healthy boundaries aren't taught; the signs of problematic people aren't taught, and the importance of listening to our intuition isn't taught (or valued), so it can be easy to wind up in an abusive relationship…but once you understand what abusive and manipulative behavior is, you won't be so vulnerable.

Ironically, those who tend to have healthy boundaries are those who have had their boundaries pushed so much for so long that they were left no choice but to go against the grain and start standing up for themselves. They learn to create healthy boundaries from necessity.

When a person has a narcissist in their life, they often second guess themselves and have a hard time figuring out the difference between normal and problematic behavior, and what's workable and what's a deal breaker. This is in large part be-cause they were continually told that the abuse either wasn't happening, or if it was, that it was their fault, or that that they were somehow the problem—that they were too sensitive, too emotional, or couldn't take a joke.

For the record, if someone hurts you or your feelings, they don't get to decide how you should feel about their behavior. If you have a problem with how you are being treated, then it's a problem, and if they continue to hurt you or your feelings, then they are not respecting you or your boundaries. If they don't care that they are hurting you, they aren't motivated to change. If they aren't motivated to change, then their behavior is going to continue. And now you have to decide what you need to do.

Whether we realize it or not, we are continually defining and redefining our boundaries with people based upon our sub-conscious standard for how we think we should be treated. The exciting thing is that once we start to get more in alignment with who we are, how we really feel, we start to become more assertive, and we start raising our standards of what we de-serve—and then (and only then) do our lives begin to radically change.

A good way to tell if your boundaries need some work is to pay attention to how you feel. If you feel irritated, frustrated, angry, or resentful, it's usually because a boundary has been crossed. If that boundary continues to be crossed, you may feel like a doormat, resentful, irritated, angry, or that others continually take advantage of you.

Boundaries can also be viewed as our "lines in the sand" or what we consider deal-breaker behavior. Boundaries can be (and often are) redrawn because as we become more in tune with our wants and needs, we learn to spend more time around people, places, and things that give us energy and less time around people, places, and things that drain our energy.

Once we quit living our lives to please others and start making ourselves a priority, we are less likely to be sucked into drama, hurt, heartache, disappointments, and one-sided relationships and friendships.

It's important to realize that when you first start setting boundaries with people who are used to doing whatever they want to you, whenever they want, they most likely will not want to be told "no." When they can't get their way, they may tell you that you are being mean, insensitive, cruel, or even abusive. Now, you might feel upset and think that you shouldn't have to set boundaries, or that others should know how to act appropriately. And I agree; however, the compassionate, caring, and cooperative people of the world must set boundaries because the controlling and selfish people of the world will steamroll over us if we don't.

The bottom line is that if you aren't comfortable saying no, then you'll have to learn to get comfortable with the consequences of always saying yes, and frankly, always saying yes will lead to sacrificing yourself to save the relationship—and no relationship is worth sacrificing yourself. These consequences of sacrificing yourself generally involve a series of one-sided friendships and relationships where you feel like a parent, a teacher, a therapist, a nurse, or a social worker always bailing out and helping this other person. You will be used and taken for granted, be treated like a doormat, become a people pleaser, and live a life full of resentment and anger that you give and give while others take and take.

When many "over-givers" start trying to set appropriate boundaries, they often confuse screaming, yelling, withholding and other types of punishing behaviors as boundary setting. This is often because they aren't okay with what's going on, but they also don't want to leave or rock the boat too much, so they stay stuck in this holding pattern of continually threatening or trying to set others straight. For many people, being assertive and setting boundaries can be intimidating, and they are afraid that this other person will react to the new boundary by breaking up or cutting them out of their lives. But if people only want you in their lives based on what they can take from you, or based on what you are willing to overlook, then there's no relationship to begin with let alone to keep in your life.

Keep in mind that your boundaries are an extension of who you are, so they are a very individual thing. Only you can decide where your boundaries are.

Here are some examples of situations and several different ways a person could potentially handle it.

Situation #1: Last year, Joan divorced a man who was a chronic cheater, liar, and who siphoned funds from her for over ten years. She recently started online dating, where she met Matt. Matt is handsome and charming and seems to have a lot going for himself. She eagerly swaps numbers with him, and they begin texting. Several texts in, Matt begins calling her "babe" and he makes little comments about how he feels like she is the one. The speed at which he is moving doesn't sit right with Joan, but she likes the attention and how focused he is on her. He's so different from her ex, who only talked about himself and was rude and arrogant. Joan isn't sure if she's making a big deal out of things or not.

Joan could:

- Say nothing to Matt and tell herself that it's just her and that she must have issues from her divorce with trusting men.

- Say nothing to Matt and wait for his behavior to really cross a line before she considers addressing it.

- Tell Matt that she's not okay with being called "babe" as they hardly know each other.

- Tell Matt that she's not okay with being called "babe" as they hardly know each other, his behavior is inappropriate, and that she thinks they need to go their separate ways.

- Instantly block Matt without saying anything to him.

Joan decides to tell Matt that she's not comfortable with him calling her "babe." Matt becomes defensive and angry and begins accusing Joan of being a typical woman who can't appreciate a good man. Because Matt showed no insight into his behavior or a willingness to respect her boundary, Joan decides that she doesn't want to see him anymore and tells him that she thinks it's best if they go their separate ways. Matt becomes enraged and begins yelling at her to not hang up on him, to which Joan decides she not only wants to end this phone call, but that she also needs to block his number and block him on social media and email.

Situation #2: Susan has been dating Marc for three months. At first things were great—ideal even. But tonight when they are having dinner at their favorite restaurant, Marc and Susan discuss politics. Susan disagrees with Marc about a certain law that just went into effect, and he launches into a tirade referring to people who think like her are "stupid and ignorant." Susan is both surprised and saddened by his behavior. She really thought he was different than the men she'd dated in the past, and that he might even be "the one."

Some options Susan might take could be:

- Say nothing and chalk up his behavior to the fact he's had a few drinks. She might think that politics is a bad dinner topic anyway and hope that he never calls her names again.

- Tell Marc that she is not okay with being talked to like that, and he must never call her names again, then see how he reacts to her drawing this boundary.

- Tell Marc that she was not okay with being called names and to get up and leave the restaurant.

Susan tells Marc that she doesn't appreciate him referring to her as "stupid and ignorant." Marc gets defensive and says that he didn't say that she was stupid and ignorant, just people in general who think along those lines. Susan decides that Marc's anger and attitude, as well as their differences in politics and world views are big enough to be deal breakers for her.

Situation #3: Ken and Tina have been married for three years. Whenever Tina's parents have a large or unexpected expense, her mother calls Tina and asks for money. This has happened numerous times and is causing conflict and resentment between her and Ken, as well as between Ken and her parents. Ken is tired of supporting her parents and has told Tina that they need to set a firm boundary as a married couple and tell her parents that they will no longer be "loaning" them anymore money. Tina feels guilty and scared about telling her mother this.

She could:

- Tell her mother nothing and hope that she doesn't ask for money again.

- Continue to give her mother money, and hope that Ken doesn't find out.

- Tell her mother that she's sorry, but they can no longer "loan" her money, and that it's causing friction in her marriage.

Tina decided to tell her mother that she's sorry, but that they've decided they will no longer be loaning people money, as it's causing friction in their marriage. Tina's mother gets very upset, and tries to use guilt, shame, obligation, and sympathy into getting Tina to cave in and give her money. Tina holds her ground and politely says "no," and then tells her mother that she needs to go now—and then ends the phone call.

Remember, your boundaries are your boundaries, and other people don't get to decide what they are. While they may want you to justify, argue, explain, or defend your boundaries, you don't need to. Your life is not a democracy, and other people don't get to vote on what you do or don't want in your life, especially when it comes to keeping yourself safe and sane.

Boundary pushes: This term refers to small or subtle words or actions that are designed to push boundaries and see how much a person can get away with. Examples include: inappropriate joking/teasing, language, touching, spending, or arriving late, name calling that is cloaked in sarcasm/teasing, claiming that they forgot about your rules/plans, etc. Emotional manipulators are masters at boundary pushing and will often do a series of small pushes that may not really register as that big of a deal at first, but confuse the target. These initial nudges will be followed by progressively larger boundary pushes. If they are called out on the larger boundary push, they may go back to smaller boundary pushes, or even good behavior, only to have yet another larger boundary push on the horizon. This is because they don't respect other people's boundaries, and they are working hard to erode them so they can get their way. Remember, it's all about them and what they want.

Boundary pushes of all sizes are often cloaked in either "It's no big deal; why are you so upset?" or "I didn't realize that my behavior was a problem." kind of attitude. And regardless of whether or not this person is an emotional manipulator, no one knows where our boundaries are unless we let them know.

Example: Brad's father is manipulative and has continually "borrowed" large sums of money from him over the years (which he has never repaid). Brad tells him that he can't afford to give him any more money. Brad's father gets upset and reminds Brad that he's his father and that family should help out other family. Brad leaves feeling guilty and selfish. Three months later, his father comes by the house and asks to borrow $20 for gas. Brad holds his boundary and reminds his father that he won't loan him any more money. Brad's father gets upset and says that it's only $20 and that he must have failed as a parent to have raised such a selfish and greedy son.

Example: Karen met Ted on an online dating site and gave him her number. At first things started off fine. However, a few text messages in, Ted began talking about sex, and certain things that he liked in bed. Karen felt like that was a little off, but she wasn't sure if she was making too big of a deal about it, as she knew the dating world had really changed since she'd last been in it. One of Karen's friends told her he was being inappropriate, especially since they hadn't even met yet, and that he seemed like a creep. But then her other friend said it wasn't that big of a deal and that maybe he was bringing up sex because he was more of a free spirit. And still her other friend thought it was very open minded and assertive of him. Karen didn't want to call things off with Ted just yet and decided to meet him for dinner.

Karen decided his flirty sex talk made her uncomfortable and asked him to stop. Ted explained that he was only talking like this because he felt a closeness to her that he rarely felt with women, but that if it bothered her, he'd stop. Karen was flattered by the closeness that he felt with her and impressed with how mature and respectful he was. She also felt bad telling him to stop and worried that she had hurt his feelings.

She told Ted that she really felt a connection to him too, but it was too soon for them to be talking about sex, and that she was looking to take things slow. Ted did stop talking about sex; however, during the first date, his conversation took an uncomfortable turn and began to focus on her body. He began complementing her on her legs and butt, telling Karen that he really liked her body, and that he could tell she worked out. Again, Karen found herself feeling uncomfortable, but wasn't sure if she was being hypersensitive or if what she was experiencing was inappropriate. All she knew was that she didn't find his comments flattering; she found them creepy. She stopped and asked herself what advice she'd give her teen-aged daughter if she was in this situation. She realized that she'd tell her teen-aged daughter that this guy was a creep and was most likely looking for sex. The more she thought about it, the more she realized that his behavior was really crossing a line and was inappropriate as they hardly knew each other—even if they'd spent hours on the phone. Karen told Ted that she didn't think they were looking for the same things and ended the date early. Ted got upset at this and said that Karen couldn't take a compliment, and that she obviously had issues with men, and that he didn't mean anything inappropriate by what he'd said. Karen just smiled, got up and left.

Brainwashing: Persuading someone to adopt radically different beliefs from their own through manipulative behavior that often involves some form of psychological abuse, such as gaslighting.

Brainwashing is usually associated with military and political interrogations, cult leaders, and religious conversions, but it is also a large part of abusive relationships and why so many targets of abuse stay. Abusive people often brainwash their targets in a slow and ongoing process, where everything that the target thinks, feels, and acts is slowly eroded or ground down and replaced with the abusive person's warped view of reality.

Example: Paula and Jim have been dating for four months, and the whole time Jim has had some "squirrelly" behavior. Paula questions Jim about his messaging other women, coming home late, and refusing to change his relationship status on Facebook from single to "in a relationship." Jim tells her that she's crazy, insecure, jealous, or has major issues. Paula never thought of herself this way before, and no other man she's dated has ever thought of her this way either. Because the good times are so good with Jim, she wants to stay. She just wishes Jim would quit acting so suspicious and guarded.

Over time, the more things Paula bring up, the more Jim criticizes her or tells her she's crazy. Her close friends are surprised and disturbed by the changes they are seeing in Paula. She now votes for the same political candidates as Jim, has the same religion and belief system as Jim, dresses how Jim wants her to dress, and has quit bringing up any concerns she has about his behavior or their relationship. She knows that there are quite a few topics that she just needs to avoid with Jim and that it's not a good idea to assert her opinions. This would upset Jim and she hates it when he gives her the silent treatment or threatens to leave her. Several years go by, and Paula is exhausted. She's tired of walking on eggshells and trying to make Jim happy and be a good girlfriend. It seems like nothing she does is enough. She's lost contact with all of her old friends and much of her family because Jim has convinced her that they are troublemakers and just jealous of their relationship. Paula feels like a shell of her former self and doesn't know who she is anymore.

Branding: Branding occurs when an abusive partner insists or pushes their partner into getting some sort of permanent marking on them (usually the narcissist's name), but it can also be some sort of identical tattoo in order to signal that they belong to them. This is usually done in the form of a tattoo, but it could be a piercing, a scarification, etc. Branding is often a one-sided request, to where the controlling partner uses guilt, obligation, fear, or sympathy in order to get their target to get a brand. For the targets who get the branding done, many mistake these permanent marks as acts of devotion, and it can take them awhile to realize that this level of devotion is very one-sided, and that their partner expects them to treat them with honesty, dignity, respect, and loyalty, but those same things are not given in return.

Example: Maria and Tony have been dating for six months when around this time Tony tells her that he'd really like Maria to get a tattoo of his name somewhere on her body—ideally on her lower stomach, her chest, or her neck. He tells her that by doing this, it would really prove to him that he can trust her, and that she's serious about him. He's already told her that his relationship with his mother wasn't good, and that all of his exes have cheated on him, and he has a hard time trusting women—and that's why he wants her to get the tattoo. While Maria's friends find Tony's behavior disturbing and controlling, Maria insists that he's not controlling—that he's caring, and because she's never experienced this level of attention and intensity before, she mistakes it for love. Maria wants her relationship with Tony to work out, and thinks that if she can just earn his trust and prove her love and devotion to him that he'll eventually soften up a bit and become less suspicious and demanding. She also doesn't want to be like every other woman who has done him wrong in the past, so she decides to get "Tony's girl" tattooed on her chest.

Codependency: This term originated in the context of Alcoholics Anonymous and was initially used to describe the excessive emotional reliance a spouse of an alcoholic has to their alcoholic partner. So the alcoholic is excessively reliant on alcohol, and the spouse is excessively reliant on the alcoholic. These relationships are one-sided; the alcoholic spouse is continually having destructive behavior, and the codependent spouse is forever busy picking up the pieces, doing damage control, and trying to make things work.

The term "codependency" has grown over the past few decades not to just reference the dynamic in an alcoholic relationship, but to include any type of one-sided dynamic. Where one person has an excessive emotional reliance on another—no matter how destructive or dangerous they might be.

The concept of codependency is often viewed as victim-blaming, as many feel that it shares the burden of the problematic behavior of the destructive person on both people involved, and doesn't take into account that the "codependent" partner is being actively manipulated or is staying due to religious, financial, or other reasons. Those who feel that way often point out that had the person realized they were being manipulated and that their partner wouldn't or couldn't change, they wouldn't have stayed for as long as they did.

Because the word codependency can feel revictimizing or victim blaming, many people shut down or get defensive if it's even mentioned as an issue. But because there are many of the elements within the concept of codependency that are so important, I think it can be helpful to put aside the word "codependency" and think about the concept in terms of "over-giving." Over-givers tend to be out of alignment with their authentic self, putting everyone else's wants, needs, and feelings first and theirs last. This is not healthy. A person who is in healthy alignment is in balance with giving and receiving. They are able to assert themselves, and they are in tune with how they feel—and they have deal breakers and boundaries for how they expect to be treated. They know it's not healthy for them to sink themselves in order to save someone else or to save a relationship.

Now not everyone who gets taken in by a narcissist is codependent, but they did have some sort of vulnerability that the narcissist was able to exploit. Whether that vulnerability was feeling lonely, scared, unloved or unimportant, or perhaps they were recently widowed or even new to town, either way, it's worth examining both your vulnerabilities as well as your "programming" about love, friendships, relationships, boundaries, and deal breakers—because you aren't cursed, or unlucky, or somehow attract all the wrong people…there is more going on here, and it's most likely on a subconscious level. In order to tell if codependency is a problem in your life, or if it was only an issue in this relationship, it's helpful to look back at other significant relationships in your life to determine if there is a pattern. If you've had several relationships or friendships that were toxic, then this isn't a coincidence, and no, you aren't cursed. The good news is that once you start examining your boundaries and vulnerabilities you become conscious of them, and can then start working towards getting more in alignment with what is healthiest for you.

Some common feelings and actions that "over-givers" have are:

-   Continually making justifications for being treated in an emotionally or physically harmful way, but would be horrified if their child or someone they loved was treated in the same way.

-   Trouble telling the difference between a healthy relationship and a dysfunctional one.

-   Feeling resentful at having to be the one to continually fix the relationship after being lied to, cheated on, stolen from, used in some way, manipulated, or from the other person being controlling and/or abusive.

-   Feeling like a parent, teacher, caregiver, or therapist to others (especially to their spouse).

-   Trouble saying no or setting and enforcing boundaries with others.

- Difficulty being assertive and instead being passive, passive-aggressive, or aggressive. Staying in friendships, jobs, or relationships that are toxic, draining or one-sided until the situation becomes unbearable.

- Feeling guilty for setting boundaries, and saying yes when they mean no.

- Feeling guilty for cutting off contact with controlling, crazy-making, destructive, disempowering, dangerous, or overall difficult people.

- Continually thinking that other people are kind, compassionate, considerate, faithful, or loyal at their core, or have the capacity to be like that—given enough love, therapy, rehab, time, understanding, or church—instead of seeing other people's behavior for what it is.

- Not setting the line in the sand when it comes to the actions of others or thinking that everything is fixable and workable and that improved communication solves everything.

- Continually trusting people who are untrustworthy and who have a pattern of lying and/or cheating.

Cognitive Dissonance: This term means "mental distress." In particular, it's the mental distress a person experiences when they have two conflicting thoughts about the same topic at the same time, as it pertains to an action that they are going to take. The reason this is so distressing is because we need our thoughts and actions to be in agreement with each other. If our thoughts and actions don't line up, then we act in a way that doesn't make sense to us, which is why we experience this mental distress. In order to relieve this mental distress, we either have to change our thoughts to match our actions, or change our actions to match our thoughts. Most of the time, we tend to change our thoughts about what we are experiencing, until it becomes problematic enough so that we have to take different actions. When we change our thoughts, we do so by either denying the problematic thoughts, or by rationalizing them.

Everyone experiences some degree of cognitive dissonance on a regular basis; however, when a person is in an abusive relationship, the degree and frequency of their cognitive dissonance is extreme. This is because their brain is continually trying to make logical sense out of illogical behavior—from both their partner and from themselves. And because of this ongoing cognitive dissonance, this is a major reason as to why they feel so emotionally exhausted.

Here's an example that I think to which most people can relate:

One morning Susan puts on her jeans. She is surprised when she finds they are really tight. She experiences cognitive dissonance when she has two conflicting thoughts: "These jeans are tight, I must have gained weight," and "These jeans are tight, but I don't think I've gained weight." Susan is mildly confused about what she's experiencing and looks for an explanation; she might tell herself that her jeans shrank in the dryer, or that they don't fit because she had a big breakfast, or that all the salt in her dinner caused bloating. If she accepts any of these rationalizations, then her actions (what she's eating or how much activity she's getting) won't change. If she tries these jeans on again in a week, and this time they won't zip, she might offer up the same excuses, or she might shift her excuses, telling herself that she's getting older and some weight gain is to be expected, or that she's put on a few pounds because of the holidays.

If she can smooth over her cognitive dissonance by continuing to rationalize what she's experiencing, she won't take a different action. Then, six months later, a friend posts a picture of them online, and Susan is shocked by what she sees: she doesn't even recognize herself. If she continues rationalizing her actions, she might tell herself that it's a bad photo, or a bad angle, or the outfit isn't flattering, and so on. She will continue rationalizing her behavior until her weight gain becomes problematic enough that she experiences enough pain, and she is motivated to do something different. It's this continual rationalization of problematic behavior that is the real problem.

Experiencing cognitive dissonance is hard enough when we are experiencing it by ourselves and about our own behavior. Things get really confusing if there's an emotional manipulator in the mix.

Here is an example:

Carla is married to Ryan. She finds out through a mutual friend that he is cheating on her. She experiences mental distress (cognitive dissonance), because she now has two conflicting thoughts: She doesn't want to stay married to a cheater, but she doesn't want to divorce Ryan. If her action is to stay married to Ryan, then she must pick a thought (and rationalize it) that is in alignment with that action so she can feel okay about staying.

While Carla is experiencing all this confusion, Ryan may deny that he cheated or depending on how much proof Carla has, he may give her a bunch of excuses, saying that the other woman threw herself at him, and that he only cheated on her once, that he was drunk when it happened, and that the other woman means nothing to him. He may blame Carla because she wasn't attentive or affectionate enough or plead that it will never happen again. He may also suggest getting into couple's counseling so they can work through things.

Since Carla still holds the thought that she doesn't want to be married to a man who cheats, but since she wants to stay married, she rationalizes his behavior. In order to do this, she may buy into any or all of his excuses (that his behavior really isn't his fault), or his promises (that this will never happen again or that he'll change).

Carla also accepts Ryan's excuses that she wasn't giving him enough affection, and that he had been unhappy for a while but didn't feel comfortable bringing up issues in their marriage. These excuses make her feel that she can change her behavior in order to change his behavior, so she can make her marriage work. Because Carla can't stay mad at Ryan, as doing so would potentially cause a divorce, she redirects her anger away from Ryan and towards the other woman. Carla blames this other woman for being a home-wrecker and for seducing Ryan. Carla also doubles up her efforts at keeping Ryan faithful and making her marriage work. (Notice how Carla is doing all the work, and all Ryan has to do is throw out enough excuses to continue to keep her on the hook.)

The problem with Carla's actions are that she can't change enough to stop Ryan from cheating. Cheating partners—especially those who have no sincere accountability or remorse for their actions—don't stop cheating, they simply learn to hide their cheating better, and generally they'll start cheating with someone new. The spouse that was cheated upon slowly becomes a physical and emotional wreck trying to convince themselves that they need to trust their untrustworthy partner, and they wear themselves out trying to save their marriage and keep their partner faithful. …And as always, in every situation where there is problematic behavior, what the other person finds out about is often only the tip of the iceberg.

In addition, if Carla's friend continues trying to tell her that Ryan is cheating, or if she isn't supporting Carla's decision to stay with Ryan, then Carla will most likely distance herself from her friend because it causes her too much mental distress to be around her.

The other major part to understanding how cognitive dissonance works is understanding that the level of mental distress experienced is in direct proportion to how emotionally invested a person is in a relationship or dynamic. The harder it is for them to walk away, and the greater lengths they will go to in order to deny or justify what they are experiencing. For example, it's a lot easier to walk away from a squirrelly business partner if you haven't invested any money yet. It's a lot harder when your life savings is on the line. It's a lot easier to walk away from a cheating or lying spouse when you don't have kids, a house, or bank accounts together. It's a lot easier to leave a cult if you haven't sold your house, given all your money to the cult, or renounced your friends and family.

Because problematic behavior tends to happen as a series of smaller boundary pushes over time, it can be really hard to see that things are a problem until they are really bad. Cognitive dissonance and the resulting justifications that occur are how people get involved with narcissists at any level—from abusive relationships, to business scams, to online dating scams, to cults, to following dictators such as Hitler—because these dynamics rarely start out as overtly problematic—if anything narcissists usually start out as a great person and, over time, slowly start to turn problematic.

In addition, most problematic behavior often happens erratically, so it can be easy (and understandable) as to how we can rationalize what we are experiencing. In the same way, abusive relationships don't usually start with a person getting cheated on, called names, yelled at, stolen from, or hit.

Keep in mind that cognitive dissonance—and many of our

rationalizations—often happen at a subconscious level, as we are often driven by either our vulnerabilities or our childhood "programming" about what is or isn't problematic.

Because it can be so incredibly difficult to think straight when we are experiencing cognitive dissonance, especially if we are emotionally invested in the outcome, this is why it's important to know our deal breaker ahead of time. This way we know what our deal breakers are; we can recognize when we are being manipulated off course—whether those manipulations come from narcissists or from friends with well-intended bad advice who push us into staying in a problematic situation. Some great ways to tell if you are experiencing cognitive dissonance is to ask yourself these questions:

- 1. If my best friend or child came to me for advice about their relationship with a person who had the kind of "strange" behavior that I am experiencing, what advice would I give to them?

- 2. If I were to ask the opinion of someone whom I thought had healthy boundaries and good judgment, what would they say about this situation?

- 3. Am I telling my friends or therapist the full truth about my partner's behavior, or am I minimizing it and only focusing on this current event and leaving out major chunks that would show a consistent pattern of problematic behavior?

- If you find yourself minimizing or rationalizing what's going on, odds are it's problematic.

Complex Post Traumatic Stress Disorder (C-PTSD): C-PTSD is similar to PTSD in that the person experiences much of the same symptoms but for different reasons. PTSD tends to happen after a specific event or situation like war or a car accident, whereas C-PTSD is more "complex" because it's often the result of ongoing traumatic events, many of which can be difficult to pinpoint. This is especially the case if a person grew up in a den of dysfunction, and the traumatizing behavior was considered normal.

Some degree of C-PTSD symptoms is common after an abusive or neglectful relationship of any kind, whether in childhood or as an adult (or both). C-PTSD is currently not in the DSM-V (Diagnostic and Statistical Manual of Mental Health, Fifth Edition), which is why so many mental health clinicians are not familiar with the term. They may diagnose a person with PTSD, or they might not diagnose what a person went through at all as any form of PTSD as emotional and verbal abuse tends to fly under the radar of what's considered problematic—especially by those who haven't been on the receiving end of it. The term C-PTSD is much more commonly used among those who specialize in emotional trauma. Having a PTSD (or C-PTSD) type response is a normal reaction to an abnormal situation and is in some ways part of the healing process as the brain attempts to piece together everything that happened into a cohesive narrative. If your symptoms are negatively impacting your life, and especially if they go on for longer than a year, it might be worth a trip to a mental health provider, ideally one who specializes in abuse, trauma, and ideally EMDR or EFT treatment.

The four main types of C-PTSD symptoms[1]:

1. Reliving or re-experiencing the event.

Memories of the traumatic event can come back at any time. You may feel the same fear and horror you did when the event took place. For example:

- You may have nightmares.

- You may feel like you are going through the event again. This is called an emotional flashback.

- You may see, hear, or smell something that causes you to relive the event. This is called a trigger, and triggers "trigger" an emotional flashback. For example, if a person has been in battle, hearing news reports, seeing an accident, hearing fireworks go off, being startled, or hearing a car backfire are common triggers for PTSD. Triggers for C-PTSD might include, feeling flashes of intense emotion (fear, rage, anxiety, crying/depression) that are disproportionate to what is going on—but you may or may not be able to connect a trigger to your intense feelings.

An example of a more direct connection would be if a person had an abusive ex that drove a red mustang, and every time they see a red mustang (even if it doesn't belong to their ex), they feel intense anxiety, rage, or sadness which might put them in a bad mood lasting hours, days, or weeks.

An example of a less direct connection would be if a person finds themselves feeling angry, defensive, and tense whenever they walk into a church, but they don't know why. They may later come to realize that they are feeling this way because as a child, their parents emotionally neglected and/or abused them, but everyone had to pretend to be a happy family every Sunday while they were at church.

2. Avoiding situations that remind you of the event.

You may find yourself avoiding talking or thinking about the event, or avoiding situations or people who trigger memories or painful feelings. For example:

-        You may avoid meeting new people (or even spending time with friends and family), because you are fearful of being hurt again.

-        You may keep very busy or avoid seeking help because it keeps you from having to think or talk about the event.

-        You may find yourself with changes in eating or sleeping (which can be ways of numbing out and avoiding).

-        You may find yourself really upset by certain music, certain restaurants, or by people who have certain features of the abusive person.

3. Negative changes in beliefs and feelings.

You may find that the way you think about yourself and others changes because of the trauma.

-        You may not have positive or loving feelings toward other people and may stay away from relationships or find yourself wanting to isolate and stay away from people in general.

-        You may forget about parts of the traumatic event or not be able to talk about them.

-        You may think the world is completely dangerous, and that no one can be trusted.

4. Feeling anxious or on "high alert" (also called hyper-arousal).

You may be jittery or always alert and on the lookout for danger. You might suddenly become angry or irritable. For example:

-       You may have a hard time sleeping, and find yourself having really vivid nightmares.

-       You may have trouble concentrating.

-       You may be startled by loud noises or sudden movements.

-       You might have a hard time trusting others—even people you previously trusted that have done you no wrong.

C-PTSD (or PTSD) can make a person feel like they are losing their mind, because they are acting in ways that seem out of character for them, and they don't know how to go back to the way they were. Please know that if you are experiencing this, you are not alone; these symptoms do tend to lessen in time, and joining a support group for narcissistic abuse can really help to better understand what you are going through.

Crazy-making: "Crazy-making" behavior is abusive and manipulative behavior that is designed to confuse, irritate, exhaust, or provoke a target into some sort of emotional reaction. The target feels either like the narcissist is trying to make them crazy, or that the narcissist's behavior is so infuriating that it's making them crazy—especially when the narcissist is acting like nothing is wrong, or that the target is making a big deal out of nothing, or worse, that the target is crazy, bipolar, or losing their mind.

Crazy-making behavior is behavior that is irrational, immature, and/or illogical. The person who exhibits this behavior tends to play dumb about their behavior, as though they don't understand what the problem is. Crazy-making behavior attempts to bait, provoke, harass, triangulate, "stir the pot," irritate, annoy, minimize, or invalidate the target often to the point where they explode in anger or become so tired of the conversation going nowhere that they give up trying to get through to them. And if and when the target does explode, the crazy maker acts shocked and confused and may use the target's reaction to further prove their point that the target is the one who is unhinged, overly emotional, or abusive.

The goal of crazy-making behavior is, in part, for the abusive person to avoid taking responsibility for their actions, as well as to keep power and control over their target (by not giving them the truth or seeking a resolution). This behavior also feeds the narcissist's ego and self-esteem, making them feel smug and superior by "winning" (controlling the conversation and pushing their target's buttons until their target reacts). It's a way for an abusive person to get and keep control over their target and over the situation.

Example: Jane continually tells John how all these other men are flirting with her, or how certain men are so attractive, and then once John starts showing signs of jealousy or insecurity, Jane spins things around, denies that she said anything wrong, and blames John for being too sensitive, jealous, controlling, and insecure. Jane takes it a step further, (because she enjoys seeing John get so upset), and in a calm and condescending voice tells him that he is jealous and insecure and needs to see a therapist.

Example: A divorced father brings back his son after the agreed-upon time, with the child not having eaten dinner or having their homework done and then acting like it's no big deal, and that they can't understand why their ex-wife is upset…or taking things a step further, and spinning things around to make themselves the target of the situation and blaming the ex-wife for not wanting them to spend time with their son.

The most telling sign that you are experiencing crazy-making behavior is that you feel like this person is making you crazy. Because crazy-making behavior is often presented in a "there's nothing wrong with what I'm doing; you are the one with the problem" kind of a way, many people on the receiving end of it become very confused as to who really has the problem. A great way to tell where the crazy-making behavior originates is to ask yourself how they would react if you were to do the same thing to them, or how others would react if they experienced it. Odds are you will find that if you were to do the same to them, they'd become outraged, or you will find that you only feel this way around certain people. If you don't feel this way around others, then it's not you, it's them.

Crumbs: Crumbs are small amounts of affection, attention, validation, or reassurance that are given in order to keep a target around so that they can continue to be used as a source of supply. Crumbs are what's usually given after the narcissist has their target hooked and begins to turn off the faucet of affection and attention—leaving the target to scramble, trying to win back their attention and affection. The reason being is because now the target has bonded to who they think is their soulmate, and they tend to think that if the attention and affection is drying up, it must be because of something they did. The target may cling to these crumbs, trying to convince themselves that these crumbs are enough to keep them emotionally "fed." However, the problem with trying to exist on crumbs is, like the saying goes, crumbs don't keep a person fed; they keep a person starving.

Here are some examples of how a narcissist uses crumbs to keep a target on the hook:

-        Telling their child (even their adult child) they love them, after making little to no effort to call, visit, or connect with them for several years.

-        Getting caught cheating and refusing to give a sincere apology, not answering any questions about their affair, or not allowing their spouse to talk to the other man/woman, but insisting that their partner trust them because they said the affair was over and their cheating is in the past.

-        Taking their child on a vacation (to a place where the narcissist wants to go). And then for the next twenty years, pointing to that trip as proof that they are a good parent and have done so much for their child.

Cycle of Narcissistic Abuse: The cycle of narcissistic abuse is most commonly known as "Idealize. Devalue. Discard." This cycle is covered in much more depth in the next section.

Dark Triad: A dangerous and oftentimes deadly combination of the three elements of narcissism, Machiavellianism, and psychopathy which results in "dark" (sinister) intent. What makes this behavior so dangerous is that a person with dark triad characteristics has a problematic degree of behavior across the board. There are the problematic personality traits of narcissism, the problematic learned manipulative traits of Machiavellianism, and the problematic brain-based characteristics of psychopathy. If you break this down, what you get is someone who uses, abuses, exploits, and/or neglects someone in order to meet their own self-esteem needs—and feels justified and entitled to act this way (narcissism), who goes about this in a way that is highly manipulative (Machiavellianism), and who cognitively lacks empathy and remorse (psychopathy). Any of these three elements by itself is problematic, however, combined with a sinister (and usually sadistic) intent, this type of person is nothing short of a predator.

Deal Breakers: Deal breakers are anything that you decide they are. For example, my deal-breaker behavior includes the "4 A's" which are abuse, active addictions, adultery, or bad attitude. (Specifically, if a person is negative, chronically unsupportive, undermining, critical, condescending, or lacking sincere accountability for their actions, this is deal-breaker behavior.)

However, anything can be a deal breaker. Some examples of potential deal breakers might be differing religions, a major age difference, a person who doesn't (or does) want children, a person who smokes, height and weight, activity level or interests, hobbies, whether or not a person eats meat or is a vegetarian, etc. Having deal breakers might feel mean or judgmental at first, but it's not. It's important that you know what you are looking for in a friend or partner—so you don't waste your time or theirs.

Just because certain behavior or preferences are a deal breaker for you, doesn't mean that this other person is bad. It doesn't mean you are bad either. It means that you know yourself well enough to recognize what you do and don't want in your life. Keep in mind that you don't need to justify your decisions about what you want or don't want in your life—especially to those that don't have to live with the consequences!

Example: Tina and Tony have been married for five years. She recently found out that he was cheating on her. He says that he's sorry, and it will never happen again, but Tina tells him that cheating is a deal breaker for her. She's glad he's sorry and that it won't happen again, but she will be filing for divorce on Monday. Tony begs and pleads, and promises to go to therapy. However, Tina holds to her boundary and tells him that his promises don't matter. She could never trust him again, and she knows herself well enough to know that if she stayed, she'd be forever distrustful, insecure, jealous, and resentful, and that she doesn't want to become that kind of person or live that way, and that's why she's divorcing him.

Example: John and Jane have been on a few dates. John begins to notice that Jane drinks more than he's comfortable with. Even though Jane doesn't drink every time they go out, and she doesn't drink past the point of being tipsy, he doesn't want to be with someone who drinks as much as she does. When he mentions it to a friend, his friend says that he's being too picky, and that most people have a few drinks on the weekend. But John doesn't care. Jane drinks more than he's comfortable with, and it's a deal breaker for him.

Example: Nancy was recently asked out by Phil. Within the first few texts, Phil began calling her "hon" and "sweetheart." This made Nancy feel not only uncomfortable but disrespected, as she hardly knew Phil, and they hardly knew each other, let alone knew each other to the level that him calling her a pet name would be appropriate. Her friends told her that it was no big deal, that they also called people "sweetie" or "honey" and that it was a term of endearment. Nancy decided that regardless of what they said, she didn't like it, and she called things off with Phil.

Example: Sally is Catholic. She meets Phil at a church function, and they really hit it off. He tells her that he's also Catholic. After a few dates he confesses that he's not really Catholic. He just said that so she'd go out with him. Sally calls things off with Phil because her faith is important to her, and it's important that she date a man of the same faith. Plus, she doesn't like the fact that Phil lied to her.

Example: Claire and Scott had been dating for a few weeks, and everything had been going great—until one night she fell asleep early. She woke up the next morning to a dozen texts and angry voice mails demanding to know where she was and accusing her of sleeping with another man. Claire was shocked at Scott's behavior and instantly called things off. Scott's rage and disrespect were instant deal breakers for her.

Diagnostic and Statistical Manual of Mental Health (DSM): This is a manual of mental disorders which is published (and continually being revised) by the American Psychiatric Association. This manual is currently in its 5th edition, and is referred to as the DSM-V. The DSM categorizes a wide range of mental health disorders, including mental illnesses, personality disorders, and developmental disorders that impair mental development.

The DSM is often referred to as the "Bible" of mental health professionals. While the different personality disorders are interesting and can lead to clarity and validation for some people, it's important to realize that diagnosing someone with a personality disorder, or even a mental illness isn't an exact science. It's more of an art, and to add more confusion to the mix, it's an art that is ever-changing.

For these reasons, I would encourage you to focus more on the behaviors and less on the labels. Behaviors are what's important. Labels change. So, even if the problematic person in your life isn't officially diagnosed with a personality disorder, it doesn't mean they don't have problematic behavior that is worthy of distancing yourself from, or being a deal breaker.

Disassociation: Disassociation is when there is a lack of connection between a person's thoughts, feelings, or actions, meaning, that they might feel, think, or act in a certain way and not know why. Disassociation happens on a spectrum ranging from mild to severe and is thought to be a psychological defense mechanism for trauma—and it's very common after a person experiences any type of traumatic event. In addition, a person can disassociate in different areas such as with time, senses, memory, emotions, environment, and/or identity.

Disassociation isn't always a bad thing, and it happens to everyone to some degree. We disassociate when we get lost in a good book or movie, when we drive home from work and don't remember how we got there, or when we are in a creative state and lose track of time for hours on end. Disassociation in a more problematic way can make a person feel like their life is a movie—and as though they are watching events happening to them, instead of experiencing them directly. When a person disassociates, they often feel numb or detached. This level of disassociation can become a problem when it's persistent, distressing, or disabling.

Dissociative amnesia (also referred to as "abuse amnesia"): Dissociative amnesia is when a person "forgets" certain incidents surrounding a traumatic event or events—in this case, abusive behavior. Abuse amnesia can ranging from "forgetting" whole episodes to certain things that are said, and the person tends to remember the abusive person in a positive light. Abuse amnesia is not normal forgetfulness, as the person is only unable to recall events surrounding the specific traumatic event. Many people who continue to go back to an abusive partner report feeling frustrated and crazy because they forget about much of the abuse and hold onto the good times...only to then be abused again.

This level of "forgetting" can really make a person question their sanity, as oftentimes they forget (or not easily remember) pretty major things.

This is such an important concept to be aware of, so you can prepare yourself for it—as this happens to the vast majority of people who have been in an abusive relationship of any kind and of any degree.

What's worked for me, and what I encourage others to do is to write out a "for when you miss him (or her) list" stating all the hurtful or hateful things they've done and then go back and read them when you are missing them, or if they try and reopen contact, and you are feeling tempted to respond. I highly recommend making this list in a bullet point format so it's quick and easy to read, because when that abuse amnesia sets in, it can set in like a strong craving and coupled with nostalgia, it can be really hard to resist. Reading your list can help keep you grounded and on track by keeping yourself away from abusive people.

Example: Kalle broke up with Derek a month ago after catching him cheating...again. The first few weeks, she was more angry than sad and vowed never to have anything to do with him again. However, by the end of the month she found herself really missing all the good times they had, and his company. She found herself thinking that maybe they could just be friends, and then sent him a text saying, "hi" and then feeling terrible about her decision to text him, and part of her hoped he would text back and part of her hoped that he wouldn't.

Example: Travis walked out on Sarah several months ago out of the clear blue. Their relationship had always been full of highs and lows, with her finding out about something Travis was up to—whether it was his chronic flirting, cheating, lying, or racking up debt she didn't know about. Whenever she mentioned any of this to him, he'd either give her the silent treatment or fly into a rage and spin things to where it was all her fault. Sarah didn't expect Travis to leave as things between them were seemingly fine, but she knew from experience that whenever he broke up with her out of the blue, that meant he was cheating on her, and that it was his way of justifying his cheating, by telling himself (and her) that they weren't in a relationship. She was hurt and angry...and vowed to herself that she wasn't going back to him. She was doing fine, until he sent her a text telling her how much he messed up and how he was wanting them to go to counseling. Sarah felt herself being pulled back into the fantasy of thinking that this time things would be different, and then pulled out her "for when you miss him" list and began reading through all the lies, cheating, hurt, heartache, and false promises of change she'd heard from Travis before. Once she reminded herself that she'd been down this road with him before, and that her experience with him had been that he didn't change—he just got better at hiding what he was up to, Sarah decided to block his number and block him on all of her social media accounts.

Dog Whistle: Dog whistle is a slang term for an indirect threat. This term comes from the concept of how a dog whistle works for a dog, meaning, when a person blows on a dog whistle to get the attention of a dog, only the dog can hear it. A dog whistle threat is done in a similar way. It's an action directed in such a way that only the target "hears" it. Dog whistle actions tend to come across as either sincere, confusing, or terrifying.

When dog whistle threats are made, they generally come across as confusing or terrifying. This is usually because the target has the feeling that they are being indirectly threatened, but because they don't have anything concrete to point to, they often feel confused, paranoid, or "crazy" and begin to doubt themselves, their perception of the situation and of this person. This is especially the case if they are trying to explain how terrifying it is to get a love letter from their ex to someone who has never been stalked or who has never encountered an abusive or obsessive person. The more they try to explain it, the more they realize how trivial it must sound to someone else, which often contributes to them feeling like they are the ones who are overreacting or paranoid.

Dog whistle threats can also come across as terrifying if the target has seen the abusive person's "mask slip" and has seen their lack of empathy and remorse, and realizes that they are dealing with a person who lacks empathy and remorse and who is capable of potentially anything.

Some examples of a dog whistle threat are:

-       A rose or note left on a former partner's windshield or on a door after the target has filed a restraining order against them.

-       A person wanting to break up with their abusive partner, and the abusive partner posting a meme on Facebook that says, "I take my vows seriously. Until death do us part."

-       An abusive person posting videos of themselves at a gun range firing at a paper target with the caption, "Practice makes perfect" shortly after their former partner broke up with them.

-       Posting quotes on social media that talk about revenge, death, violence or other types of harmful acts, commitment or love being forever, or otherwise settling the score.

Domestic Violence: The United States Department of Justice defines domestic violence as, "a pattern of abusive behavior in any relationship that is used by one partner to gain or maintain power and control over another intimate partner. Domestic violence can be physical, sexual, emotional, financial, or psychological actions or threats of actions that influence another person."

Domestic violence does not only include married couples, it can be any harm inflicted on a member of a household or family by another member of the same household or family.

Example: Martha's mother has been verbally, emotionally, and physically abusive to her and her two brothers since they were small children. However, Martha is the one who bears the brunt of her abuse. Anytime Martha shows any individuality that doesn't line up with her mother's view of her, her mother verbally and emotionally undermines her, by saying her goals or plans are wrong, stupid, or complete fantasy, and that she'll never achieve them.

Example: When John's father left his mother for another woman, John's mother, Eve, began referring to John as the man of the house, even though he was only seven. Eve would pressure John to sleep in the same bed as her and cuddle and listen to her vent whenever she had a problem. As John got older, Eve guilted him out of having friends or dating, by telling him that she was scared he would run off and not come back home too—and that she didn't know what she would do without him. John felt bad for his mother and didn't want her to feel anxious like that, and over time, he ended up sacrificing all of his friendships and plans to go to college so he could take care of his mother.

Example: Paul was controlling, demanding, and temperamental. His wife, Sharron, and two children walked on eggshells around him. He would periodically explode and launch into verbally abusive tirades, cussing at them and calling them names. Periodically, his temper would escalate to where he began shoving his wife or his oldest son around the house. Neither Sharron nor his son viewed what was happening as abusive, since they weren't being hit. It wasn't until Sharron began seeing a therapist for anxiety that she learned that she was, in fact, in an abusive relationship.

Example: Serena's mother would discipline her children by either whipping them with a belt until they couldn't sit down, or she would lock them in the closet with the light off until she decided they'd had enough. She continually told them that she did this because she loved them and just wanted them to behave.

Enabling: Actions that are taken, usually with the intention of helping a person or saving a relationship, but that result in further harm—generally because the "help" (enabling behavior) only helps the person continue making problematic choices, as well as avoiding natural consequences for their actions.

An example of enabling behavior would be a parent who allows their adult child, who is an alcoholic, to continue living in their home without paying rent, doing chores, or helping out in any way. They may also not say anything when their child comes home drunk, or they might buy their child alcohol, as they want to avoid the fight they know will ensue.

The result to the person that is being enabled is often harmful because, in order for most people to be motivated to change what they are doing, they have to experience enough pain to do something different. Stopping enabling behavior can be difficult, as the enabler is often being manipulated with guilt, obligation, pity, or fear of what might happen to the person if they don't continue to care for them.

Abusive people need enablers around them so that they can continue acting abusively. Friends, family members, certain children, and their spouses are often enablers, offering up excuses and minimizing the abusive behavior until they realize that this person is in fact abusive, and that there is no excuse for it.

Enablers often give similar excuses as the abusive person, claiming that they had a bad day, were stressed out, had a bad childhood, were provoked, were drunk, tired, etc. It's important to realize that there is no excuse for abuse.

Example: Diane confronted her boyfriend, Ted, about him cheating on her. Ted became enraged and denied everything, then spun things around and blamed Diane for snooping and being jealous and crazy. The more Ted refused to be accountable for his cheating, the more enraged Diane became. At some point in their fight, Ted grabbed a knife and stabbed Diane in the shoulder and in the leg. Diane was able to call 911 and made it to the hospital, and Ted was arrested. When Ted's mother heard about what happened, she blamed the police and Diane for overreacting and said that Ted didn't deserve to go to jail as he was obviously not trying to kill her because he only stabbed Diane in the shoulder and in the leg. Ted's mother then rallied other family members to raise funds to help Ted post bail.

Example: Tina was the adult child of a verbally abusive father who would often fly into a rage for the smallest reasons. Her mother and sister had justified and tolerated (enabling) his behavior for decades by blaming his behavior on his bad childhood, and then spinning things around to make Tina the one with the problem, claiming that she needed to be more compassionate and understanding. Tina told them that she was no longer going to be treated this way by him, and that if he yelled at her again, he would no longer be welcome in her home or around her children. Tina's sister and mother were horrified that she would set boundaries with her father, but no matter how much guilt they tried to put on her, Tina held her ground and explained that she was not his emotional punching bag, and that she will no longer tolerate being treated like that—by anyone, regardless of who they are—even if they are family.

Emotional Flashback: The concept of an emotional flashback is commonly associated with sudden and intense emotions of fear, anger/rage, or despair that seem to appear out of nowhere and are disproportionate to the situation.

However, the concept of emotional flashback can also work the same with intense positive emotions as well. They can feel like a sudden and intense pleasant emotion, such as love, joy, comfort, or happiness that seems to appear out of nowhere and is disproportionate to the situation.

I feel it's important to extend the concept of emotional flashback to cover positive emotions as well because, regardless of whether the emotion is pleasant or unpleasant, if a person is taking action based on either pleasant or unpleasant triggers and emotions from past events, the results can be problematic—because they aren't seeing the situation for what it is. In either type of emotional flashback, a person may or may not be able to pinpoint why they are feeling this way. Sometimes, the cause (trigger) is more direct, and sometimes, it's indirect.

Emotional flashbacks generally don't happen like they do in the movies. In the movies, a person literally (and vividly) "flashes back" to the event itself and details of a full scene replay in slow motion. For many people, emotional flashbacks don't happen this way. If anything, they are often experienced as a brief flash of intense emotion that doesn't seem to line up with what's currently happening. These feelings may disappear as suddenly as they appear.

Some people might experience emotional flashbacks as a more intense emotion and know exactly where it's coming from. The feeling may stay with them for hours, days, or longer. Every person is different, and every emotional flashback is different. People can (and generally do) have multiple types of emotional flashbacks, all with different degrees of intensity.

Most people experience emotional flashbacks of some sort and to some degree, although they might not make the connection between their current feelings and a past event. Unpleasant emotional flashbacks can (understandably) cause a person a tremendous amount of emotional pain and upset. For that reason, they may go out of their way to avoid certain things that they know trigger them, and that's okay.

However, I think it's really important to mention that because emotional flashbacks can be so painful and persistent, a person can start to feel as though they are at war with their own mind. This can be such a terrible and isolating feeling especially if they don't realize that they can be triggered by people, places, events, or sights and smells that are normally positive, such as a baby laughing, receiving a gift, or hearing Christmas music.

Example of an unpleasant direct emotional flashback: Roger is listening to the radio when the Van Halen song, "Panama," comes on. In an instant he is emotionally brought back to his prom night in 1984, where this song was playing in his car right before they were hit by a drunk driver, which killed his best friend. A wave of intense sadness consumes Roger, and he begins to sob. His reaction catches him off guard because he thought he'd dealt with his friend's death and didn't realize all these feelings were there, let alone still so intense.

Sometimes when people experience an emotional flashback, they aren't taken back to the event itself, but to the emotion that they felt during that event. For example, Roger may remember that "Panama" was part of his prom night, but he may not realize that it was so directly tied to his friend's death. The intense sadness that he experiences may really catch him off guard. He may realize that it's connected to his memory of his friend, and once he stops crying, he may think everything is fine. However, he may find himself in an emotional funk that could last hours, days, or even weeks, and he may not know why.

Example of an unpleasant indirect emotional flashback: Every time James drives past a church or when anything relating to religion is brought up, he feels intense anger. For decades, he thought his intense dislike and anger towards religion was because he thought religion was ridiculous and unnecessary.

However, when he attends his niece's wedding, he is surprised by his overwhelming anger as he walks into the church. He is bothered by how intense this emotion is, and realizes there had to be more going on than just his issue with organized religion. After thinking about it for the rest of the weekend, he realizes that his anger comes from his childhood, where he was forced to go to church with his parents every weekend and play the part of the loving and happy son in a loving and happy family. While, in reality, his parents spent the week abusing and neglecting him. He realizes now that church was a trigger, but the emotional flash backs of anger and resentment that followed were due to his dynamic with his parents.

Pleasant emotional flashbacks can come across like feelings of an immediate connection or fondness towards a total stranger because they remind us of other times, places, or people with whom we felt a fondness. They can be a subconscious driver of our decisions, and it's important to bring to our awareness as much of what's going on in our subconscious as possible. It can be problematic if we feel an immediate intimate connection with someone that we don't know because they look like someone else we know (or maybe don't look like them, but have the same name) and don't realize that a real connection isn't there.

Example: Tina meets Don through an online dating site. When they meet for coffee, Don shows up driving the same type of classic pickup truck as her deceased father, whom she adored. Immediately, she is overwhelmed with positive emotion and feels an intense (and unfounded) degree of closeness with Don.

Example: John meets Susan who looks a lot like Elizabeth, a girl he dated in high school. He instantly feels attracted to her. After dating for about four months, he realizes that they don't have a lot in common and that he doesn't really like her. He realizes that his feelings stem from the fact Susan reminds him of Elizabeth and all the good feelings and the strong connection that was there between them. John is shocked by this realization and understands that he needs to see Susan for who she is, then make a decision about whether to keep dating her based on their chemistry and compatibility and not based on how he felt about Elizabeth thirty years ago.

Example: Simone meets Joan, a financial planner. As soon as she shakes her hand, she catches the scent of her perfume, which is the same as what her favorite teacher in 7th grade used to wear. She immediately feels a sense of trust, connection, and safety with Joan and is quick to agree to her ideas about how to invest her money.

Fleas: This concept comes from the saying, "lying down with dogs will give you fleas." This is not the most flattering term, but it accurately describes how many of us "pick up" unhealthy behavior patterns and habits from being in or around a dysfunctional person or environment.

These unhealthy behavior patterns can be picked up from having dysfunctional behavior role modeled when a person was young, and/or "fleas" could also be the coping skills a person had to develop in order to function the best they could in a dysfunctional environment. After being in a relationship with a narcissistic person, many people feel like they've taken on some of the same problematic behaviors. This often scares them and makes them wonder if they have somehow become a narcissist too.

Fleas can be physical or emotional responses to situations. They can be directed toward the narcissistic person or they can be directed toward others. But, once you become aware the problematic behavior, you can work towards changing. The concept of fleas is not an excuse for problematic behavior, but it can go a long way in helping a person to understand why they are doing things that they feel are really out of character, or that are out of alignment with the kind of person they want to be. The good news is that once we know better, then we can start to do better.

If you are concerned about your behavior, then at least you have an awareness that you need to work on some things. An awareness that there is a problem is the first step in working towards changing that behavior. So, if have concerns about your behavior and are motivated to change it, then go for it.

The difference between narcissists and people with fleas, is that narcissists don't (sincerely) think there is anything wrong with their behavior. They don't spend any time on introspection and wondering if their behavior could be the problem. They feel entitled and justified in using, abusing, exploiting, or neglecting others in order to get their needs met whereas people with fleas are often upset and scared of their behavior and sincerely want to change it.

Some examples of fleas are:

- Brian grew up with an abusive father. Even though he swore to himself he'd never be like him, he found himself yelling at his kids the same way his father yelled at him. Brian's behavior greatly upset him, and he was horrified that he was turning into his father. He decided to start going to therapy on a regular basis so that he could break the cycle.

- Barbara was married to Ryan, who has repeatedly cheated on her. The first time this happened, they went to counseling, and she thought they worked through any issues that they had— and that he wouldn't cheat again. Ten years later, she discovered that he had not only been cheating again, but that he had never stopped—and had even gotten another woman pregnant. Barbara was devastated and enraged. As usual, Ryan promised he would change, and then blamed Barbara for not being committed enough because she no longer wanted to work things out and wanted a divorce. Barbara decided to stay married to Ryan because she didn't believe in divorce. However, in order to cope with staying married, she began drinking, abusing prescription anxiety medication, and began having an affair with a male coworker. Barbara and her friends were concerned about her behavior, but Barbara was so full of anger and resentment, she felt the only way she could stay would be to numb out and settle the score.

- Don grew up with narcissistic parents who gave him gifts that felt like an afterthought. Their gifts were impersonal and showed they really didn't know him. Sometimes, the gifts were given weeks late which enforced in him the idea that he didn't matter. Don learned early on to mask any feelings of disappointment, hurt, or anger, or else he was told he was ungrateful, too sensitive, difficult, or too demanding. Don grew up feeling very tense and anxious around birthdays and holidays, as they were always disappointing and full of pain—pain that he was never allowed to express. As an adult he avoids celebrating special occasions, and when he can't avoid a holiday or birthday, he finds himself giving really impersonal or thoughtless gifts to others. He gets upset with himself for waiting until the last minute and giving gifts that aren't reflective of how he really feels about the person.

Flying Monkeys (also called "abuse by proxy"): This term comes from the movie, "The Wizard of Oz," where the Wicked Witch of the East has flying monkeys under her spell to do her bidding, which is mainly to harass and torment Dorothy and her friends. In terms of a narcissistic relationship, "flying monkeys" are people who have been manipulated by the narcissist in order to carry out their bidding, usually to harass and torment the narcissist's target, or to push them back into the relationship.

Anyone can be turned into a flying monkey—friends and

family of the narcissist, friends and family of their target, therapists, members of their church, and/or neighbors; you name it. Because they are also being manipulated, flying monkeys are duped by the narcissist into believing that either the narcissist is the victim of the situation, and the target is the one who is manipulative and abusive, or that their relationship issues are somehow shared issues (which they are not). As a quick side note, saying the relationship issues between a narcissist and their target are shared issues, is a lot like saying the dynamic between a bully and their target are shared issues, and that the target is partially to blame. Or that the problematic dynamic between a cult leader and a cult member is due to communication issues. Open, honest, sincere, solutions-oriented communication with a narcissist does not stop them from bullying or taking control away from their targets—if anything, having open, honest, sincere, and solutions-oriented communication often makes things worse, as the narcissist isn't looking for a solution, they are looking to use, abuse, exploit their target. The more they know their behavior is working to grind their target down, the more they will either do it, or they will change their approach in how they do it.

The narcissist's bidding generally includes spying and getting information from the target, pushing the target back into the relationship, stalking, harassing, or abusing the target.

Example: Teri was verbally and emotionally abusive to her girlfriend Jane. Jane thought that given enough time, love, and therapy Teri could change, but she didn't. The final straw for Jane was when she found out that Teri had been cheating on her...again. A few weeks after their breakup, Jane started to get dirty looks from people and found out that Teri flipped everything around and told their friends a bunch of lies about her, saying that Jane cheated on her, and that Jane was abusive. Jane is shocked. Several of their mutual "friends" started to leave nasty messages on her phone and through social media. One night, while she was out for dinner, Jane's car is keyed.

Example: Rachel divorces John after years of his physical and verbal abuse, which included name calling, yelling, belittling, shoving, throwing things, and threatening her. John begins telling their mutual friends that he never abused her, that he might have raised his voice a few times and said a few things he regrets, but that he never hit her, or cheated on her. After minimizing his behavior, he then spins things around and makes himself the victim of Rachel. John claims that Rachel is just a gold digger and only married him for his money, and now she's trying to keep him from his kids. His friends and family start treating her terribly and take up John's cause as their own. They fight for him to get full custody of the children because they believe Rachel is an unfit, manipulative, and abusive mother.

Example: Raul and Samantha are Christian, fairly active in their church, and have been married for thirty years. Raul has cheated, lied, and siphoned funds from their joint account multiple times. Samantha has finally had enough. She has been through all of his excuses, lies, and promises to change enough times now that she realizes he's not going to change. She files for divorce. Once Raul gets the papers and realizes Samantha is serious, he goes to their pastor in tears, telling him that he has a sex addiction, and that all his lying and stealing is because he strayed from God. He begs for help to save his marriage and to find his way back to God. Raul says he'll do whatever it takes. He joins different men's groups in the church and tells anyone who will listen his tale of woe and how he's working so hard to turn his life around because it damaged his marriage and hurt the woman he loves. Everyone in their church begins to view him as a sheep that has strayed from the flock, but now has seen the error of his ways, and who has found God. The congregation and the pastor start encouraging Samantha to give him another chance. They can tell he really means it. The pastor calls Samantha and encourages couples' counseling with him (which, unbeknownst to the pastor, has now made Raul's individual issues into relationship issues and the pastor is now revictimizing Samantha by having her share the blame for Raul's behavior). Due to all this pressure, Samantha caves in and gives Raul another chance. The pastor and the congregation are all thrilled with themselves for helping Raul to find God and for keeping the couple together. Raul is on his best behavior for a while, and things seemed to have really turned a corner…until Samantha's coworker tells her that she came across Raul's profile on a dating site.

Future Faking: This is when a narcissist talks about, hints at, or promises their target an ideal future together. The narcissist may future fake by claiming that they want the same things from the relationship, or promise to change their abusive behavior.

Narcissists often go about future faking by gathering information about the target's idea of a great future or perfect relationship from the early love-bombing stage, which often includes getting engaged or married, buying a home, settling down, starting a business, moving to a different area in order to get a fresh start (from their bad behavior), adopting pets or children, having a baby, or some other false promise (or worse, they actually do these things) in order to manipulate the target into a new relationship or into rekindling a broken relationship.

At first these actions may seem sincere. After all, who would talk about such deep commitments if they weren't sincere? The narcissist may even turn their talk into actions and convince their target to buy a house, adopt a pet or a child, or move, and over time, the target may realize that they have become more trapped as a result of these actions—trapped because they now have a mortgage they can't afford alone, or have started fostering (or adopting) a child, quit their job and moved, or otherwise committed themselves to the promise of doing these things as a team. Then they realize that the narcissist isn't emotionally invested, and so the target stays out of guilt, obligation, or the inability to undo these actions.

What started out as the promise of an ideal future quickly turns into a hellish nightmare.

Example: Scott and Diane had only been on a few dates when Diane began feeling an intense soul-mate connection to Scott. They seemed to have so much in common, from the types of movies and music they liked, to having a similar sense of humor and what they did for fun to being entrepreneurial and loving big city life. A few weeks into dating, Scott began hinting about moving to New York and starting a restaurant. He also began talking about how great it would be if they ended up getting serious and starting a family someday as they both wanted to home school their children. Diane had never felt this way about anyone, and even though all this talk about marriage, children, moving to New York, and starting a restaurant seemed too soon, it felt so right. She decided to make the jump, and paid to move both her and Scott out to New York.

They quickly found an old restaurant for sale, and Diane took out a large loan to fix it up and open shop. Shortly after they rehabbed and opened up the new restaurant, Scott's behavior began to change. He began showing up late, and when he was there, he was often flirting with the waitresses or customers. Diane began to wonder if she'd made a mistake by combining her life with Scott. She brought up her concerns with him, and he denied his behavior, saying that he was just being friendly and social. Several months later, she found hidden credit card statements from credit cards Scott had opened up in the business' name, showing that they owed quite a bit of money—none of which she knew anything about, and none of which were for business expenses. When she went home that night to confront him about it, she found he had cleaned out their apartment and drained their bank accounts. Diane began to realize that Scott had sold her on a dream and delivered a nightmare.

Example: Dave had caught Samantha cheating…again. When he confronted her about it, she said that it was because he'd been working late and hadn't been spending enough time with her. She also blamed the guy (Jerry) that she'd been cheating with, saying that he'd been pursuing her relentlessly at work and finally wore her down. Even though this was the third time he'd caught her cheating, Dave wanted to believe that things could be fixed between them. After all, Samantha seemed really sorry. She vowed that she'd do whatever it took to earn his trust back, and was an ideal partner for the past two weeks. Last night, she suggested that they renew their wedding vows. Dave was thrilled, but his friends were not. Samantha said they needed a fresh start, and that Dave needed to quit being around people who weren't supportive of them. She suggested that after they renewed their vows, they could start over by moving to the country like Dave had always wanted.

Example: Ryan and Lee recently broke up due to Lee's cheating and lying. In an attempt to keep Ryan in the relationship, Lee is on his best behavior, and even schedules couples' counseling for them. Things are going great in counseling, and they are going on date nights. Ryan is shocked at how quickly Lee's behavior turned around and is thrilled that they seemed to have found such a skilled therapist, as he's seeing such massive change, and in only two visits! Lee promises to do whatever it takes to make things better. He insists that they have such an intense connection that he just can't walk away, and he now sees what he's done wrong and wants to be the man that Lee deserves. For Christmas, Lee gives Ryan a puppy, and they post happy pictures of them together with this puppy all over Facebook, which makes Lee look like the ideal partner, and Ryan lucky to have him.

Gaslighting: The term "gaslighting" is taken from a 1944 movie, called "Gas Light," starring Ingrid Bergman. In the film, Bergman plays the part of Paula, a woman who is married to Gregory, a man who unbeknownst to her is a thief and the murderer of her rich aunt. Little does she know that Gregory only married her so that he could have access to her aunt's house so that he can find her aunt's jewels—which he was unable to find in his earlier robbery attempt. Whenever Gregory is hunting in the attic for the jewels, he has the gas lights on (the movie takes place in a time before electricity). Since the lights are on in the attic, it causes the rest of the lights in the house to flicker. When Paula asks Gregory why the lights are flickering, he tells her that they aren't, and that this is yet another sign that points to her being "crazy." As Paula begins to uncover things about Gregory that don't line up, and in an effort to being found out by her or others, he slowly begins to erode Paula's perception of reality (and sanity) by moving objects around as well as telling her that she is not well whenever she questions what is happening.

Today, gaslighting is a slang term that refers to a form of psychological abuse in which information is twisted, spun, or selectively omitted to favor the abuser, or false information is presented with the intent of making targets doubt their own memory, perception, and sanity. It is commonly used with narcissists and other types of emotional manipulators who are either trying to avoid being accountable for their behavior, or who are intentionally trying to erode their target's sanity. Gaslighting is incredibly damaging and crazy-making behavior, which often has long-lasting results and leaves a person questioning their sanity and perception of reality not only when they are around the abusive person, but in general.

Example: On their second date, Tina asks Paul if he has any children, and he says that he has one, a daughter who lives with his ex-wife. Several months into dating, Tina comes across a picture online of Paul with three children. When she asks him about it, he says that those are his children. Tina is confused and tells him that she thought he'd said that he only had one child. Paul gives her a confused look, and tells her that she must have misheard him, or is misremembering. He tells her that he has three children and has never told her anything different. Tina says that she distinctly remembers him telling her that he only had one child. Paul begins to get upset and asks Tina, "Why would I have told you that I have one child, when I have three? That doesn't make any sense. I'm starting to think you might be nuts and need a therapist." Tina becomes embarrassed and self-conscious, and agrees that it doesn't make any sense for Paul to lie about something like that, and so she accepts his explanation that she misheard him, or misremembered what he'd said.

Example: Janet and Roger have been married for five years, and while Janet was doing the laundry, she found a receipt for condoms in the pocket of Roger's jeans. She shows him the receipt and asks if he's cheating. Roger grabs the receipt out of her hand and tells her that it isn't for condoms, but for candy and that apparently Janet can't read—and must be looking for a fight. Then, he tears the receipt into pieces and throws it in the trash. Enraged, he spins the focus of the argument onto Janet by accusing her of having trust issues and being jealous. Janet begins to wonder if perhaps she did read the receipt wrong. While she is lost in confusion, Roger then spins the conversation to make himself the victim, by telling Janet how he does so much for her and complains that all he gets are accusations in return. Janet is caught off balance by his response and finds herself apologizing for questioning him. She begins to wonder if she really is jealous and unappreciative. Roger tells her that if she doesn't get some therapy, he's going to leave and find someone who isn't so jealous and insecure.

Gaslighting doesn't have to be done over a long period of time to cause devastating long-lasting effects on a person's sense of reality. Even when done a few times, it can erode a person's sense of faith in their judgment and in their perception of people and of reality, often to the point where they really struggle with trusting anyone or anything–even friends, family, their day-to-day decision-making, or their overall perception of reality. And when a person is told something they know to be true isn't true (especially repeatedly), they soon begin to doubt themselves and look to others (oftentimes the abusive person) for confirmation of what's is happening.

Examples:

- A spouse claiming that the person they are sending flirty messages to is only a friend and that they are jealous and crazy for thinking otherwise.

- A boyfriend (or girlfriend) hiding their partner's car keys in order to make them late to a job interview, and then pretending not to know what happened to the keys.

- A spouse abusing their partner and then denying that it ever happened.

Grand Finale: This is a term used to describe an over-the-top ending of a relationship with a narcissist which is often characterized by an extreme amount of drama, chaos, lies, and overall outrageous, soap-opera type of behavior. Their behavior can be so extreme, that it can quickly become dangerous—even deadly. The target of any abusive person needs to use extreme caution when leaving the relationship, even if the narcissist has never shown any signs of violent behavior before, because once the narcissist realizes they've lost power and control over their target, they begin to scramble and say or do anything that they can in order to get that power back. It's around this time that the narcissist's mask either slips, or is taken off completely, and the target is shocked by what they see. They may be shocked by the level of contempt the narcissist has for them and realize that the narcissist does not love them or even like them. This can be a hard reality to accept and leaves many targets feeling numb and angry once they realize the narcissist is nothing more than an emotional con artist—and someone they don't even know (because they don't), and feeling used, abused, and exploited (because they were).

Example: Shannon and Mark had been married for ten years. During these ten years Shannon continually felt frustrated and outraged with Mark's financial irresponsibility, his addiction to porn and frequent trips to strip clubs, his chronic lying, his put downs, and his continual indifference about his behavior and its impact on her. She recently found out that he had been flirting with a woman through text messages. When Shannon confronted him about this and asked him if he was cheating, Mark denied it and told her she was paranoid, jealous, and crazy, and that he couldn't take these accusations. He insisted that he had female friends and that's all this other woman was. Then the other woman, Rachel, contacted Shannon, and it turned out that Rachel was pregnant. Confronted with Rachel's pregnancy, Mark said that they'd only had sex once, and it was during a time that he and Shannon had been fighting. He claimed that this Rachel meant nothing to him and that he would do anything to save their marriage, begging to give him another chance and for them to get into couple's counseling. Mark seemed to say all the right things, and even the counselor thought they were making progress. Shannon's best friend wasn't buying it and encouraged Shannon to talk to Rachel, to get her side of the story. Shannon told Mark that she wanted to meet with Rachel, and after many fights about it, Mark reluctantly agreed. Then he came home and said that Rachel was too embarrassed and ashamed to meet with Shannon, but that she'd be okay with texting. Mark gave Shannon Rachel's number, and they began texting. Sure enough, Rachel confirmed everything in Mark's story. Rachel even said that Mark had told her how much he loved Shannon and that she was a lucky woman. Shannon believed the texts, until one night when she sent Rachel a text while Mark was in the bathroom. She heard a strange sound in Mark's jacket. It was text notification, but not his normal one. She sent a few more texts, and sure enough his phone kept chiming. She went into his jacket and saw that he'd bought a cheap phone, and that she'd never been texting Rachel—she'd been texting Mark all along!

That was the final straw for Shannon. She moved out that night. Over the next few months, she found out who the real Rachel was, and the two of them began to uncover lie after lie that Mark had told each of them. The more of the truth that came out, the more ridiculous the situation became. She found out about hidden bank accounts, other women, and debt she never knew about. She learned of lies he'd told other people, including that she'd had cancer and that's why he'd stayed with her, and that he had tried to leave her before, but she continually manipulated him into coming back claiming she needed him because of her illness. Rachel even showed Shannon a text saying that he thought his son with Shannon wasn't really his! Rachel told her that Mark had vigorously pursued her, and that the only reason he was pretending to work things out with Shannon was so that he could divorce her and not get screwed over financially. Shannon could hardly believe that this was her life, or that Mark could have been capable of so many lies and such a jaw-dropping level of deceit, disrespect, and disregard for her and their marriage. Mark's behavior was so outrageous that Sharon felt like she was living a soap opera!

Gray Rock: Gray rock is a technique used to minimize contact and damage from a narcissist by becoming as emotionally unreactive and boring as a "gray rock." The goal with using the gray rock technique is to stay cool, calm, collected, uninterested, and uninteresting when around a narcissist so that they lose interest in abusing their target and stop. There is a saying out there that goes, "Violence is only enjoyable when there is suffering. Without suffering it is a hollow act." The goal with gray rock is to not let the abusive person see you suffer. By denying them this, you are cutting off the "supply" they are getting from your pain.

This tactic flies in the face of most thinking behind conflict resolution, which is based around having open, honest, sincere, solutions-oriented communication. The reason this type of communication doesn't work with a narcissist is that they are not looking for a solution—they are looking to bully their target. Let me be very clear: to let an abusive person know how much they are hurting you, will only make the abuse worse, as they now know they are getting to you—and worse, they specifically know what buttons to push. It's dangerous to treat an abusive relationship as though the issue has to do with communication issues between two people. It doesn't. The issues are about power and control, and the abusive person is intentionally grinding their target down. They know damn well what they are doing, so don't get caught up thinking that they don't, or that if you could just somehow explain to them how much they are hurting you that they would stop. Again, this will only make things worse.

It can be really difficult not to be reactive when an abusive person is actively bullying, harassing, and overall attacking you. But keep in mind that their abuse is all a game to them—and they play to win. Any reaction, no matter how small, can suck you back into their twisted and highly manipulative game. And they will often provoke their target until the target explodes—at which point they use the target's reaction as proof that the target is crazy, bipolar, or abusive. If they can provoke their target into reacting in front of others or through text or email, then they can then use their reaction to prove (to others and even a judge) how unbalanced the other person really is, thereby strengthening their (skewed) position that they are the victim of their target.

So why do they provoke and bully? They do this because it's their way of trying to hold onto power and control over their target, because doing so makes them feel smug and superior.

This game is only fun for them if there is a reaction, and if the target does not respond or does not react in the way that the manipulator hopes, then they usually become bored and leave the target alone. However, if they bully you ten times, and you even respond once, it may be enough for them to keep at it.

The goal with gray rock is to shift from being reacting to responding.

Becoming emotionally unreactive takes practice because emotional manipulators are really good at knocking people off balance—and that's exactly what they are trying to do. The more you can anticipate what they might do and plan your responses ahead of time, the better off you will be. Manipulators know exactly what they are doing, even though they pretend not to. Continually pointing out to them how their actions are hurtful, angering, or crazy-making in an attempt to work towards improving communication or working towards a resolution is a mistake. They are not solutions oriented. They are looking to get and keep power and control over their target. Letting them know that they are hurting you will only add fuel to the fire.

Gray rock is used when a person must keep contact with a narcissist for whatever reason, but the ideal form of interaction with a narcissist is no interaction (which is called "no contact"), or minimal interaction (which is called "low contact").

Gray rock is done by either ignoring a narcissist's attacks completely, or if you must see them, being brief, keeping the topic of the conversation at a surface level, and staying emotionally neutral—similar to how you might talk to a stranger in an elevator.

I feel it's also important to add that while gray rock works for most people, you and only you know your situation the best. If you feel that going gray rock is going to make things worse or put you in danger, then do some modified form of it to where you can keep yourself safe.

Example: Susan's ex-boyfriend, Paul, had contacted her six months after they broke up asking for a paternity test for their child. Their court order stipulated that Paul was not to contact Susan directly but to go through her attorney. Paul's email made Susan livid. Not only was he questioning the paternity of their child (especially since he had been the one cheating on her), but he was contacting her directly, which he wasn't supposed to be doing. Susan knew that he was emailing her in order to provoke her to become angry and reactive. She initially wanted to send a letter letting him know what an unbelievable jerk he was, and how he was the one cheating, and how dare he question the paternity of their son, or go against their court order, but she didn't give him the satisfaction of seeing her get upset. She also was half tempted to forward his email to her attorney, but then decided to delete it instead. After all, the court order read that he was to contact her attorney, and he didn't, so why should she have to jump through the hoops to make his requests known? She decided that if he really wanted this test done, he needed to contact her attorney like the judge had ordered.

Example: Kara had recently dumped John out of the clear blue (and in the most nonchalant way) after two years of dating. John was devastated, but his friends were thrilled she was gone, as she was nothing but drama—she was constantly trying to make John jealous and even going so far as to flirt with them or other guys at the bar in order to get John upset. To John, these nights out with her were so predictable and usually a no-win situation. Either she expected him to get into a fight with these men who were flirting with her—which would get him thrown out of the bar, or if he didn't get into a fight, she'd get upset and claim that he didn't care about her, and then freeze him out emotionally and physically.

Things between Kara and John's friends were so bad that they refused to hang out with him if she was going to be around. Within two weeks of her ending things, Kara had plastered pictures of her getting engaged in Hawaii to her new boyfriend all over Facebook. It was a trip that she and John had planned! John couldn't believe what he was seeing and that Kara could move on so fast—like what they had never mattered, or even happened. He felt that on some level Kara had posted these pictures to hurt him, and he didn't want to give her the satisfaction, so he didn't say anything about it to any of their shared friends, as he knew it would get back to her. Instead, he vented to his therapist.

Grooming: This is a term that describes what the goal of certain abusive, controlling, and boundary-pushing type behavior is designed to do, which is to "groom" the target into behaving a certain way. "Grooming" a target is done in a wide variety of ways, but perhaps the three of the most common ways are a narcissist giving the target the silent treatment after the target confronts them about some sort of "squirrelly" or problematic behavior; threatening to break up or divorce them (or actually breaking up) if the target doesn't act in a certain way, or by planting seeds that they will leave if they act like a supposed ex acted.

Example: George caught his girlfriend Linda texting other men. When he confronted her about this, she refused to acknowledge it or have a conversation about it. Instead she got upset and acted like he was the one who had done her wrong, and she gave him the silent treatment for over a week. The silence was unbearable, and George felt like he was in limbo. He didn't know if he was ever going to hear from Linda again. During her silent treatment, he continued to text and call her, begging for her to talk to him, and apologizing to her…even though he did nothing wrong. He was saying anything in an attempt to get her to talk to him and to try and make their relationship work. Linda did eventually reopen communication with George, and although George didn't readily realize it, Linda had groomed him into never bringing up any issues he had with her texting other men.

Example: Dawn and Larry had been married for ten years. During this time, whenever Dawn brought up any issue she had with Larry—his yelling, put downs, or controlling demands of her time and how she dressed, Larry would fly into a rage and threaten to leave or divorce her, claiming that she was manipulative, controlling, and abusive. Although Dawn didn't readily realize it, Larry had groomed her into never bringing up any issues she had with him. He also was gaslighting her and making her question her sanity and her perception of events.

Example: Susan had been dating Mark for about three weeks. During this time, they began talking about their previous relationships and their exes. Mark told Susan that he had a lot of female friends, and that his ex was incredibly jealous about this. He told Susan that he broke up with his ex because she didn't like that he spent time with his female friends, and he couldn't stand how controlling she was. He went on to say that he was so glad he'd met Susan, as she didn't seem crazy and jealous like his ex. Initially, Susan didn't have an issue with Mark being friends with other women, as she had several male friends from college she still saw periodically. However, Mark's female friends didn't seem to be just casual friends, as they were all single, and he liked many of their sexy pictures on Facebook. Because Susan didn't want to be seen as jealous and controlling like Mark's ex, she didn't bring up any of her issues about Mark's "friendship" with these other women. Although

Susan didn't readily realize it, Mark had groomed her from the beginning to never question his (very questionable) dynamic with his "female friends."

Hoovering: A manipulative technique named after the Hoover vacuum, where the narcissist attempts to reopen communication with their target with the intention of either fully sucking them back into the relationship or sucking them back into their "supply pipeline" by keeping communication open, so the narcissist could re-enter their life down the road in order to use, abuse, or exploit them.

Hoovering consists of any attempt to reopen communication with the target, no matter how small and seemingly innocent. Hoovering is often done in the form of text messages, phone calls, liking comments or pictures on social media, emails, contact through mutual friends, family, children, neighbors, coworkers, or "accidentally" bumping into the target. Multiple forms of manipulative messages can be used, from seemingly kind, considerate, or harmless attempts at communication (where they might claim to just want to say, "Hi," "Happy Birthday," or "I love you") to more aggressive or provoking messages such as claiming that they have cancer or some severe illness, or even making suicide threats in order to get the target to respond.

When most people get a seemingly innocent and friendly hoover, they are usually caught off guard...and knocked off balance. This is usually due to two main reasons. First, the narcissist seems friendly and nonchalant, as though the narcissist doesn't realize that they aren't on good terms. Second, because the message seems innocent and friendly which causes confusion, and the target has trouble with deciding how to respond. They might feel incredibly angry that the narcissist is contacting them, or emotionally wounded because they are still trying to heal from the relationship. They may also feel guilty, rude, or over-reacting by ignoring the message, so they cave in and respond, thinking that responding once can't do any harm. And that's exactly how these hoovers are designed to make a target feel. After all, most people would feel panicked and saddened if someone texted them saying they were suicidal or had cancer. However, most of the time when a narcissist says these things, they are nothing more than another lie in their long string of lies. You do not need to respond. Remember; they are abusive, they are not your friend, and they are trying to manipulate you. You don't owe them anything. If they truly do need help or someone to talk to, they need to turn to someone else—and the reality is that they would…if they really needed help. If you are getting messages with them claiming to be suicidal, you don't need to respond—you can call 911 (or whatever the number to emergency services is in your area) and have them respond. Frankly, this is the best way to handle suicidal messages for three reasons. First, because emergency responders are trained to handle suicidal people, and second, because if they aren't serious about being suicidal, they will quickly learn that you won't be manipulated by messages like this, and third, because the narcissist may also be homicidal, and may have plans on taking you out, or taking you out with them if they really are suicidal as well.

Any response to a hoover reopens communication which will inevitably start the cycle of abuse again. Hoovers often lead back to the "idealize" stage of a narcissistically abusive relationship, where the target finds themselves believing that perhaps this time the manipulator really has changed, or that things weren't that bad, or that their issues really can be solved.

Some examples of a hoover:

"Hey there, Happy Birthday. Thinking of you."

"I can't take this anymore. You mean the world to me. I'm going to kill myself if you don't answer this text."

"My mother was just diagnosed with cancer, and I really need to talk to you."

"I just realized that I left some stuff at the house. Can I come by and get it?"

"Merry Christmas."

"You ruined my life. All I ever wanted was to be with you. I hope seeing me suffer makes you happy."

"I'm sorry things didn't work out. You are really such an amazing person, and I'm tired of hurting you. You deserve better."

"I know you may not ever want to talk to me again, but I really need your help."

"I can't feel my left arm. Is this what a heart attack feels like?"

"I miss you."

"My new girlfriend (or boyfriend) is allergic to pets. Can you take the cat?"

"I'm sorry. You were the best thing that ever happened to me, and I'll do whatever it takes to earn your trust. Can we go to therapy?"

Ingratiating Behavior: Ingratiating behavior is when a person tries to get on someone's good side through the use of flattery or people-pleasing type behavior. It is very common for targets of abusive people to use ingratiating behavior in an attempt to get the abuse to stop or to try and "earn" being treated nicely.

Example: Joan works for a woman who is controlling, intimidating, and often flat-out mean. In an effort to get into her boss' good graces (and to avoid being a target of her abuse), Joan makes it a point to compliment her every chance she gets.

Example: Tom is verbally and emotionally abusive to his daughter Kathy. In an attempt to try and have a workable relationship with her father, Kathy attempts to both walk on eggshells and not bring up topics that have in the past upset Tom in any way (such as any issue she has with how he mistreats her, or any topic in which they don't agree on in general). Instead, she pours her energy into being what she thinks is being a good daughter. She cooks, cleans, does his laundry, never disagrees with him, and never questions or challenges him in any way. However, no matter how much she twists herself into an emotional pretzel, and tries to please her father, it is never enough, and it doesn't stop his abusive treatment of her.

Inner Child: I know this concept may sound hippy woo-woo to some people out there, but understanding it is a very large part of what it means to truly heal from narcissistic abuse. The concept of an inner child isn't just adults learning how to have fun again (although that's part of it). On a bigger level, reconnecting with your inner child means to reconnect with your authentic self—usually the self that has been damaged or lost through negative messages or experiences in childhood.

Many of those damaging messages can come from either abusive, or well-intended (but still dysfunctional) parents, as well as they can (and also do) come from the dysfunction in society as a whole—whether it's TV, movies, oppressive religious beliefs, oppressive gender roles, culture as a whole, peers, teachers—and anything that serves to separate a person from who they really are. Both men and women have an inner child, and by the time a person has reached adulthood, everyone has received some sort of problematic programming about who they are supposed to be, and what they are capable of...even if they had a great childhood. Most of us don't question this programming because we don't realize it's a problem—we are on autopilot, and tend to think that our way of doing things is the right way. It's often about midlife that a person starts to realize that they've been a living a life that's been expected of them, and not the life that brings them joy.

Getting in touch with your inner child is an ongoing process, and the first step involves getting in tune with how you feel. Because when you reconnect with who you really are, you are in alignment with not only your thoughts and feelings, but also your likes and dislikes, and what you want to do in this life.

One exercise that has helped me get back in tune with my authentic self has been to start thinking about how I feel about people, places, events, or "stuff" in my life on a number scale ranging from 0-10, with 0 meaning "ice cold" and 10 meaning "I love it!" This exercise may sound totally unrelated and flat-out weird, but trust me; I think you'll find that it's very eye-opening. The purpose of this exercise is to get in tune with how you feel about everything around you, and then to probe a little deeper and ask yourself why you gave the number that you did. (This exercise is not an exact science, and the number you give will most likely change over time as you grow and change.)

I've found it's easiest to start assigning a number to items to which you don't have an intense emotional investment. So for example, I started with items in my kitchen. I have some hand-blown drinking glasses that I got when I lived in the Southwest that I love. Those are easily a "10" for me. My dishes are around a "7" and my pots were a "3." The reason my pots were a 3, is because they were scratched-up Teflon, which is toxic, and made me cringe every time I used them. What's interesting is that feeling that cringey feeling had become so normal to me, I didn't realize how many negative emotions I had surrounding cooking! Once I realized this, I got rid of those pots and pans and bought a stainless steel set which are now a "10" for me.

By the end of this exercise, I realized that I had a lot of things in my life that were below a 7. Once I realized something was below a 7, I would stop and ask myself what needed to happen in order to make this a 9 or 10. Sometimes that meant I needed to donate the item and replace it with something that was a 9 or 10, and sometimes it meant something as simple as moving it to another area in my house.

This exercise can get really interesting when you start assigning numbers to your relationships, friendships, and job situation— and you may find that some major changes need to be made. Those changes might include spending more time with certain people, and less time with others. It may mean asking your boss if you can do more tasks that you enjoy, and less that you don't. It may mean rearranging your office to make it more relaxing, or it may mean quitting your job and finding something that is a better fit.

Living a life that is enjoyable starts with first getting in tune with what is (and isn't) enjoyable--and your authentic self, your inner child, knows what is enjoyable. If you find yourself get-ting stuck, or caught up in indecision, another way to approach this is to find the objects or relationship dynamics that are a 3 or less. Once you know what you don't want, or what feels "bad" or "off," then by default, you know some elements of what you do want and what feels good.

A good life isn't one where everything is going good all the time, or only reserved for weekends, vacations, or retirement, or something that happens down the road after you heal, or after you make more money, or after you get divorced. A large part of living a good life is living an authentic life and being able to authentically express yourself in small ways every day.

Isolation: Isolation is the number one tool in a narcissist's tool kit. Isolation can be done in many different ways, but here are three of the main ones:

- Love bombing the target to where they only have time for the narcissist (which oftentimes the target becomes intoxicated with this level of attention and affection and may only want to spend time with the narcissist).

- Moving a person physically away from their friends and family.

- Insisting or encouraging the target not to spend time with their friends or family claiming that they are a bad influence or jealous.

In addition, the target may also find themselves wanting to isolate from others when their partner's problematic behavior starts surfacing (especially if it's reoccurring). They may feel embarrassed and ashamed about what is going on, and how they are treated, so they may quit talking to friends and family about what's happening—or they may minimize much of what's happening. Isolation may occur if friends and family have distanced themselves from the target because they either couldn't emotionally handle watching the target be in an abusive relationship, or because the friends and family are resentful or hurt that the target didn't make them a priority while they were in a relationship with the narcissist, but now that the relationship is over they want to spend time with them.

Isolation usually also occurs after the relationship, due to PTSD and feelings of anxiety, depression, and paranoia. If you are in a relationship where you are finding yourself minimizing how you are being treated, or if your partner is wanting you to cut ties with friends and family, then this is abuse, and it's a problem.

If you are recently out of an abusive relationship and are finding yourself without a support system, I highly recommend joining a website called meetup.com and joining a dozen or two groups that even sound remotely interesting to you. You don't have to go to every event, but the more groups you join, the more options you have, and you may find yourself meeting some great people and doing some fun things you would have never thought of doing before.

Low Contact: Low contact is the alternative to "no contact" and is usually done if a person wants or needs to keep communication open with a narcissist. For instance, a person might want to stay in minimal contact with a family member who is a narcissist, or they may need to stay in minimal contact if a person has a child with a narcissist.

Low contact is whatever amount of contact that you want it to be. You may decide that you can handle seeing this problematic person only for three days over the holidays, or you may decide that you can't do three days, but you could do one day—or maybe that one day is too much, but meeting for dinner is fine, or if that's too much, perhaps limiting contact to a phone call on holidays or a couple of times a year.

A great way to tell how much contact to have with a person is to examine how you feel when you are around them, and after you are around them. If you feel angry, resentful, hurt, annoyed, or that you need to decompress after being around them, then these are all signals that something needs to change. Either some boundaries need to be set for how you expect to be treated; the length of time you are spending with them might need to decrease, or you might need to increase your self-care when you are around them or after you are around them…or some combination of all three.

If a person has to keep in contact with an emotional manipulator, they can do a combination of low contact and "gray rock"— so when they (infrequently) have to see them, they also stay emotionally neutral and unreactive as possible.

Example: John's mother has consistently ruined every holiday since he was a child. She either creates a scene, starts a fight, or criticizes his life choices. John has only kept a relationship with his mother out of a sense of obligation. He has come to the point where he is tired of her behavior and has decided that he won't fly home to spend time with her this Christmas—that he will call her instead.

Example: Chad and Sue are divorced. Originally, Sue thought they could divorce and be on decent terms. This has not been the case. Chad continues to text and call her with messages that are demanding, obsessive, and accusing her of being a whore and seeing other men. Chad also stops by the house at all hours of the day and night, claiming that he wants to talk to her or to see their daughter without regard to her or their daughter's schedule. Sue decides that she doesn't want (or need) to talk to Chad about anything other than their daughter, so she arranges it with her attorney that from here on out, all communication from him needs to go through the court, as well as a parenting plan needs to be developed. So while Sue's daughter may have a relationship with Chad, Sue realized that she didn't need to continue to be exposed to his abuse and went as low contact with him as possible.

Love Bombing: Love bombing is when a narcissist "bombs" their target with "love," or more specifically, attention, affection, communication, and compliments. Love bombing is a term that is usually (and originally) associated with cults and how they go about recruiting members; however, the same concept is used by narcissists regardless of the role they play in a person's life, whether that is as a cult leader, an abusive partner or parent, an online-dating scammer (or scam artist in general), a coworker, neighbor, etc.

Love bombing often leads to rushed intimacy, heavy amounts of "mirroring," a whirlwind romance, a high degree of future faking, and a feeling of a soul mate connection.

Love bombing tends to start off very fast, where the narcissist is spending hours every day talking, messaging, or spending time with their target. The narcissist is often very quick (within the first week or two) to start hinting or saying that they have a soulmate connection with their target, and that they love them, or that they are so glad to have finally found them. The constant compliments, communication, and soulmate connection, can make a target feel loved and appreciated—and for someone who is starved out emotionally, love bombing can feel intoxicating or even addicting. Because love bombing can feel so "right," a target rarely sees anything wrong with how fast things are moving—although they might have some concerns that things are a little too good to be true. More often than not, the target is thrilled to spend hours upon hours every day communicating with this person and soon making them their whole life…and will be defensive and start distancing themselves from anyone who is concerned about how fast things are moving, or who has concerns about this new person in their life.

What makes love bombing so dangerous and effective, is that the narcissist is not only isolating them from their support system so they can make them their whole world, but the target is willingly going along with distancing themselves from their support system. And because love bombing can feel like the start of the most ideal situation or relationship, it can be really difficult for a person to see it as problematic, and to walk away from it—or to even want to slow things down. After all, it can be really hard to walk away from someone who is coming across like the ideal partner who wants to live the ideal life with you.

For all these reasons, love bombing often goes hand-in-hand with the first stage in the cycle of narcissistic abuse, which runs the course of "idealize, devalue, discard." Love bombing not only happens when a narcissist first spots their target, but it also often happens each time the target tries to leave the relationship. And again, it can be very hard to walk away from a person who either promises to change and says all the right things, or who is seemingly taking massive action to change such as going to therapy, church, or rehab (but who is really learning that they need to hide their double life better). A relationship or dynamic with a narcissist often has a high degree of intensity and over-the-top behavior that during the love bombing phase can feel like a fairy tale, and during the discard stage can feel like a nightmare.

Many former targets of narcissists want to warn the new target, and if they try to they will often find that the new target doesn't believe them, and instead gets defensive and maybe even joins in with the narcissist on a smear campaign against the former target. After all, during this love bombing/idealize stage, it's really hard to believe that Prince (or Princess) Charming is actually their worst nightmare.

Another point about love bombing that I think is important to address, is that to the former target, all the love bombing that the new target is getting can seem like perhaps the narcissist really did find true love—and maybe the former target really was the problem all along, because after all, they seem so happy and perfect together. This is because the new target is going through the love bombing phase, and odds are the narcissist will devalue them in very much the same way—because healthy people do not love bomb, they do not rush intimacy, and they do not move at lightning speed.

Also keep in mind, that if the narcissist is making a grand effort to show you (or the world on Facebook or other social media) how perfect their new life is with their new partner, they are doing so in large part to further grind you down—which is part of the continuation of the devalue and discard cycle you are in with them. So, to a narcissist, it's a triple win. They get the satisfaction of grinding down their former target, love bombing their new target, and then getting all of their enablers and fan club to rally around them and their new-found great relationship—because after all, odds are that the narcissist has been painting themselves as a victim of you this whole time.

Two last points about love bombing that I really want to drive home. First, is that even people who have been caught up with love bombing before, still have a hard time walking away from it (or slowing things down) because oftentimes they are afraid that maybe this time it's the real thing, and they don't want to lose a potential soul mate just because they've been previously burned. This is especially the case if they were in a relationship with an overt narcissist. If a person has had an overt narcissist in their life, who was an absolutely selfish, controlling, verbally-abusive jerk, and then they are love bombed by a narcissist who comes across as attentive and overly romantic, this kind of over-the-top behavior can really seem like ideal and healthy behavior.

Second, a lot of people struggle with intense feelings of depression and numbness after a relationship with a narcissist. They find themselves wondering if they'll ever "love" or be "loved" like this again—especially if they are starting to date again. It's normal to mistake love bombing for love, because it is so intense, but it's not real. And real love can't compete with the intensity and theatrics that make up love bombing. So please know that those excessive gestures of love bombing by the narcissist are not love; they are manipulation, and those intense feelings that are created by all the highs and lows are also not love or "chemistry," or a soul mate connection; they are trauma bonds that are created by the highs and lows of their behavior. Once you can see love bombing as all smoke and mirrors designed to suck you in, it is easier to walk away. Real love is based on appreciation, caring, concern, and the desire for the other person to be happy and fulfilled. Real love takes time to develop, and it makes a person feel safe, secure, valued, and appreciated. It does not make a person feel emotionally devastated, anxious, unhinged, depressed, or suicidal, and it does not include abuse.

If you are dating again, please go at a comfortable pace. If you are feeling concerned or confused by any behavior you are experiencing, then these are signs to take some steps back both physically and emotionally until you can see clearly. There is no downside to taking things slow. If a person truly respects you, they will respect your boundaries too.

And, as always, if you feel like something is off, it's because something is off.

Example: Sarah met John through an online dating site and after a few texts, things really began to pick up steam. Sarah was shocked at how much they had in common and how much John wanted the same things out of life that she did. They seemed to be so on the same page that Sarah felt she'd met her soul mate. They began talking and texting for close to six hours every day. Soon, she didn't have time for anything or anyone else outside of work and John, but she was more than happy to make John her whole world. Everything just felt so right. She was becoming almost addicted to hearing from him, and within the first two weeks John told her that he loved her and wanted to marry her. Sarah was flattered, but she was also concerned, as she felt John's professions of love seemed really immature, and not something an adult would say or feel—after all, they'd only known each other for a few weeks. Sarah told John that she felt they were moving a little too fast, and that she didn't think he knew her well enough to love her. John told her that he felt the way he felt, and instead of telling Sarah "I love you," he began telling her "As you wish," which was code for "I love you"—a line that came from her favorite movie, "The Princess Bride." Sarah thought John's intensity was sweet, and she felt so loved and important by all the attention he was giving her.

Some of Sarah's friends were concerned with how much time she was spending with John and how fast things were moving.

Sarah became defensive of her relationship, and told herself that they were jealous or had issues with men, and she began to withdraw (isolate) from them.

Example: Susan had decided that online dating was a haven for perverts and weirdos, so she decided that from here on out she was only going to meet men the old-fashioned way—in real life. She was thrilled when she met Scott at church several weeks later. After a few conversations, things began to pick up quickly. Scott texted Susan throughout the day, from good-morning texts, good-afternoon texts, to good-night texts, and several dozen texts in between. When she'd get home they would skype for a few hours while she was making dinner so they could catch up on each other's day. They had much in common, and Susan found herself telling Scott things that she wouldn't normally tell a person she hardly knew. Even though she'd only been talking to him for about two weeks, he didn't feel like a stranger. If anything, he felt like her best friend or soul mate. The amount of time she spent communicating with Scott was a little concerning for her, but at the same time, it was refreshing because her last boyfriend wasn't attentive at all and only texted her when he was bored or horny. She brushed her concerns aside, telling herself that she needed to appreciate a good man—after all, how many women would complain that their boyfriend was too good to them? She chalked up her hesitation and concern by telling herself that maybe she'd never experienced real love before, and that was why this relationship felt so "off." After three months of dating, Scott moved in with Susan, and that's when she began to see some of his controlling and abusive behavior. Susan felt emotionally deflated. She'd been down this road before and knew she needed to break up with Scott, but she also knew how difficult it was most likely going to be to get him out of her house.

Example: Ryan and Rachel had been married for two years. During this time, Rachel had seen flashes of problematic behavior from Ryan, all of which she chalked up to either his culture or his stress at work. It wasn't until they had their first child that his behavior escalated, and he became very verbally abusive. She couldn't believe the switch in his personality. It was like living with Dr. Jekyll and Mr. Hyde, and she never knew which side was going to surface. At first, she (and her friends and family) chalked up his behavior to the stress and lack of sleep with the new baby. But even when her mother babysat to give them some time alone, he would still lash out at Rachel. Rachel finally told Ryan that couldn't handle his yelling and name calling anymore, and that she was taking the children and moving out. The next day Rachel came home to a candlelit dinner, flowers, and a sign that said, "I love you." It was so romantic and thoughtful that Rachel unpacked her bags and gave Ryan another chance. Rachel's best friend Sarah (who had been in an abusive relationship and who had gone through something very similar) pointed out that while he did all these nice things, he never actually apologized or was fully accountable for his behavior. Rachel knew that Sarah was right, but she wanted to believe that maybe this time Ryan had seen the light and that their relationship was actually turning a corner. She became angry with Sarah, and told her that if he didn't care at all he wouldn't go to these great efforts to try to keep their family together. Sarah replied that Ryan's grand efforts weren't love, that they were love bombing, and that he wasn't being sincere, he was being manipulative.

Manipulative Behavior (I CHIVE): Narcissists want what they want when they want it, and they will often do whatever it takes to get it. The main ways they go about manipulating are by what I call, "I CHIVE" which stands for: Isolation, Charm, Hope, Intimidation, Violence, and Emotion (which includes fear, love, obligation, and guilt).

Here are some examples of each of these types of manipulative behaviors in motion:

Isolation: Moving the target away from friends and family by wanting to spend all their time with only them, or by discouraging them from spending time with others (specifically those who have a problem with their abusive behavior).

Charm: Apologizing, saying all the right things, using humor or seduction to make light of the abuse, promising to do whatever it takes to fix the damage from their behavior, promising a great future together, love bombing.

Intimidation: Threatening divorce, or to not pay child support, or to hurt them or those they care about if they don't do what they want.

Violence/Aggression: Yelling, cussing, throwing items, pushing, hitting, hitting or shoving items around the person.

Emotion (fear, obligation, guilt): This is where a narcissist manipulates a target's emotions in order to get them to stay.

Fear: Giving an ultimatum (either stated or implied) that if the target does (or doesn't) do something, some sort of major consequences will happen, such as threatening not to pay child support, or threatening to hurt the target, the children, or the target's friends or family. Other examples of inciting fear in the target would be throwing items near the target, punching holes in walls, or talking about death (or dreams that they had of the target being in an accident, disappearing, or dying).

Love: Doing grand, romantic displays (love bombing) in order to win the target back. These sweeping gestures often create or reinforce the intense, soul mate connection their target feels towards the narcissist.

Obligation: "I can't believe you're so quick to leave this relationship—doesn't commitment mean anything to you?" Or, "The kids need two parents. I can't believe you are doing this to them."

Guilt: "How can you leave me at a time like this?" or, "You owe it to the children to stay and work things out," or, "A real Christian/Muslim/Hindu/Buddhist (etc.) would forgive. I expected more from you," or, "I guess you are perfect and never make mistakes." or, "You know how hard it is for me to admit that I need help...and I need your help right now. I want to change, I just don't know how."

Masks of a Narcissist: This refers to the different faces (or masks) that a narcissist shows in public as well as to the target—especially in the beginning. These different masks are often socially acceptable and ideal which can make them seem charming, likable...and the furthest thing from an abusive person. When a narcissist switches masks, or when the mask slips, their true self is seen, which is often very horrifying and different than the person the target knows. Over time, the narcissist's mask slips more and more often, and the target starts to view the narcissist as having a "Dr. Jekyll and Mr. Hyde" personality, or having both really great and really awful sides to themselves.

Some of the masks they wear might be that of the great parent, the God-loving church-goer, the volunteer, the world's best spouse, or the charming and funny person. However, those close to the narcissist know that many times their actions are very different than those of the people that they pretend to be.

When a narcissist's mask slips, it is usually only the target who sees this—at least at first. The more the narcissist knows that their target won't leave, the more often their mask comes off, to where they may stop hiding their abusive behavior and become comfortable acting this way in public or in front of friends and family.

Because abusive behavior is often behavior that is disproportionate to the current situation, many people, including the target, are confused by what is going on. And because of this, they often justify as the abusive person having a bad day, being under a lot of stress, being tired, how the narcissist was raised, or that the target must have done something to cause them to act this way.

When a mask slips, or comes off completely, the narcissist's true self, which is composed of deception, manipulation, and cold, calloused, or calculating behavior is revealed. Many targets are terrified of the person they really see when the mask slips and often describe them as dark, terrifying, or evil. At this point, the narcissist may (or may not) try to get their mask back on— and quickly switch back to a nice, caring person, (which isn't sincere—it's just more manipulation). When their mask continues to slip, (which tends to happen if they are being confronted with lie after lie) it's as though they are completely unraveling. They might go from professions of love, to threats of violence, to trying to be friendly, to crying, to yelling, to apologizing, to claiming they are hearing voices, or that they are suicidal, or even that they have cancer. When none of that works, and they realize that they have "lost," they become enraged, and there are no more masks. Their complete lack of empathy and remorse is what their target often sees.

It can be absolutely mind boggling and terrifying to see a narcissist go from love bombing and professing that you are the love of their life, to seeing their mask slip and realizing that they don't love you—that they don't even like you and could potentially harm or kill you and feel totally entitled and justified in doing so.

Example: Raul and Maria had been married for five years. During this time, Raul was charming, likable, and came across to Maria and most other people as the world's greatest husband. However, once they had their first child, Raul became verbally and emotionally abusive. It was like a switch had flipped. Maria had never seen this side of him before, at least not to this extent. At first, she chalked it up to stress about the new baby, but as time went on his behavior got worse. At Thanksgiving, he began cussing and yelling at her for not cutting the pumpkin pie in the right way. She was embarrassed and ashamed by the scene that he caused and apologized profusely. All of the family and friends who witnessed this scene felt awkward and ended up leaving early. Raul called them all the next day, being his charming, likable self and apologized for his behavior and blamed it on holiday stress and alcohol. Everyone except for Maria's aunt Marge who'd been in an abusive relationship before, was quick to forgive him and seemed impressed with how accountable he was for his problematic behavior. Marge wasn't impressed at all. She was concerned for Maria as she saw right through Raul's mask and fake apology.

Mask (of Narcissist) Coming Off: A narcissist will generally take off their mask completely when they realize that their target fully sees them for the manipulative liar that they are. It is during this time that the target is in the greatest amount of danger, and the narcissist is no longer pretending to care, and worse, because the narcissist lacks empathy and remorse and feels entitled to treat their target in whatever way they want, things can escalate really quickly. When the target sees the emotional manipulator for what they really are, they are usually terrified and are concerned that they might be in danger (which they might be).

Example: After being married to Raul for seven years, Maria was done. She was tired of riding the roller coaster of his Dr. Jekyll and Mr. Hyde moods and enduring the verbal and emotional abuse and apologies that followed. She filed for divorce and served Raul papers. He flew into a rage in front of their neighbors and their children. He didn't even try to hide his abusive behavior. Even though Raul didn't make any direct threats towards her or the children, she was terrified by his actions…and the look in his eyes. He had this cold, dark look, and Maria felt as though she was seeing the devil himself. She'd never seen anything like that before in him or in anyone else, and she felt like he could kill her and the children and not even think twice about it. After he left the house, she realized that she and the children needed to leave immediately and never go back. She called the police to come and do a civil stand-by, in case Raul came back because she was fearful of being in the house alone with him.

Example: Sandra found out that her boyfriend, Al, was cheating on her. When she confronted him about it, he became incredibly angry, not only because she was accusing him of cheating but because she'd been going through his phone and seen the text messages from another woman. He flew into a rage, and began yelling, cussing, shoving, slapping, and hitting her, blaming her for looking at his phone, and telling her that she was the one who couldn't be trusted. Sandra and Al had fought before, but never this like this. She was terrified by what was going on. He didn't even look like himself—it was like he was possessed. Sandra found herself apologizing over and over again in an attempt to get him to stop yelling and hitting her. Her neighbors heard their fighting, and called the police, who then arrested him. As the police were taking Al away, he screamed at her, "Look at what you did you psycho bitch! I hope you're happy! You ruined my life! I'll get you for this!" He had this cold, dead, crazed look in his eyes, and Sandra was terrified that he'd kill her if he ever saw her again.

Narc Speak: This term is short for "narcissist speak," and generally refers to a series of either misleading, loosely-related, or nonsensical words that a narcissist will string together in an effort to avoid accountability, and groom their target into not questioning or challenging them in any way. Like the rest of a narcissist's behavior, narc speak is about gaining and keeping control over the situation, their target, and their target's perception of reality.

You may also hear the term "narc speak" being referred to as "word salad." However, it's important to know that there are two types of word salad. On a medical level, the term "word salad" is generally used to describe the disorganized speech (which includes loose associations and resulting bizarre word combinations) that can happen from cognitive impairment due to schizophrenia, Alzheimer's, a stroke, or other type of brain injury or mental illness. This is not the same type of word salad in which narcissists engage.

The difference between "medical" word salad and a narcissist's word salad, is that medical reasons for word salad are due to a cognitive issue; whereas, with narcissists it's due to a personality issue. When a person suffers from a cognitive form of word salad, it is not intentional; it's generally ongoing and happens regardless of the topic brought up. The person with word salad usually struggles to make themselves clear, and their disorganized speech may improve with medication or time. Narc speak type word salad is intentional (it's their attempt to manipulate), it isn't pervasive through all of their speech, it tends to only happen when they are trying to avoid accountability, or gain control, and they don't strive to make themselves more clear—if anything the conversation gets more confusing and frustrating the more they speak, and medication or time don't impact their behavior in any positive way.

While narc speak is often "word salad," it can also be any form of communication that doesn't make sense or is the opposite of what's actually happening. Narc speak is crazy-making, and often leaves those who experience it feeling frustrated, exhausted, and confused because they are usually working overtime trying to make sense of a nonsensical conversation. They often spend a lot of energy trying to get through to the narcissist, and to get the conversation back on topic, thinking that a lack of communication is the issue—which it's not. The narcissist isn't trying to reach an understanding; they are trying to confuse and detract from the original issue at hand. In short, the narcissist is trying to keep control over the situation and the target by not giving them the clarity that they need.

Narc speak often involves a narcissist talking in circles, not staying on topic, or just flat out not making sense. An added layer to the crazy-making can be when the narcissist blames them for not being able to communicate effectively or for the conversation getting derailed or not reaching a resolution. Narc speak often leaves a person wondering what on earth just happened. The conversations are so confusing and exhausting, that during one, the target often gets burned out and just wants the madness to stop—but then often spends hours or days rehashing what was said in an attempt to untangle it, as well as trying to formulate reactions to all the points that they didn't get addressed. These conversations are often such a mishmash of unrelated points, that the target has a hard time articulating what just happened or what was even said to friends or others, often describing it as "A bunch of craziness," or "The conversation went nowhere...as usual."

Here are some different ways narc speak is done:

Saying one thing but meaning another. When a narcissist is using narc speak to mislead, they may say one thing to keep their target on the hook but actually mean the opposite. Unfortunately, the only way to really tell if a person is saying the exact opposite of what they are intending (or doing) is after a person has experienced a pattern although, sometimes this behavior does raise a red flag. You might get the feeling that someone is trying too hard to convince you of their intentions—especially if they are speaking in such certain terms shortly after you've gotten to know them. As a side note, people who are telling the truth assume that they will be believed; they don't try to convince others they are telling the truth or of their intentions.

Examples:

Narc speak: "Trust me. I would never hurt you."

Translation: "You can't trust me. I am going to hurt you."

Narc speak: "I love you."

Translation: "I don't love you, I just want you to think I love you because it keeps you around so I can continue to use, abuse, and exploit you for my own selfish reasons."

Narc speak: "I will do what it takes to earn your trust back."

Translation: "I want you to think I'm dedicated to rebuilding trust, so I'm going to tell you anything I think you need to hear, and maybe I'll be on my best behavior for awhile if that's what it takes to keep you sucked in. Nothing I say will be the complete truth, but you should be grateful that I'm even willing to discuss any of this, as frankly, I feel entitled to do whatever I want and you just need to deal with it—because we both know that you aren't going to leave. If you need additional proof about what I'm doing, or what I did, I won't give it to you, because then you might leave. I'll get upset and tell you that you are living in the past or bringing up old issues and keep pushing you to trust me and to never question me. And if you have a hard time trusting me (which you should), then I'll make you feel like you are the one who is jealous, insecure, and has issues with trust."

Random words and phrases strung together. These types of conversations generally happen when a narcissist gets knocked off balance by being confronted with the truth and they scramble to regain control. What tends to come out of their mouth is a mishmash of excuses, lies, and random words, all strung together in a frantic attempt to regain control over the conversation (and of their target).

Example: Mary catches Jim in a string of lies and confronts him about it:

Jim: You took all that the wrong way, but I think you were looking for a way to diminish this and an excuse to leave. I respect your choice, but I think you should take a look at that if you really want to find love.

Mary: What exactly did I take wrong?

Jim: Whatever you perceived in my text that would provoke you to give up on something with this much potential so quickly.

Mary: You mean all the small lies?

Jim: Tell me exactly what it was that made you decide you should give up on us?

Mary: All the small lies.

Jim: All in jest. The crux of humor. There is no plural to that word. I am not a liar, but I do understand that your past and the way it looked on the text. I understand how you feel and I respect your choice. I wish you nothing but the best.

"Plausible Denial," as in the good old Bill Clinton type. I refer to this as the "semantic shuffle," as they choose their words very carefully to where the shuffling of one or two words can change the meaning of what they are saying completely. For example, they might say something like, "There IS no relationship with that woman" instead if "There WAS no relationship with that woman." On the surface, it may seem like they are denying having a relationship with "that woman," but that's not what they are saying. What they are saying that currently there is no relationship with her, not that there never was a relationship.

They redefine words and concepts in order to convince themselves and others that they aren't a liar. For example, a narcissist might say, "I was never involved with that woman" and in their mind, since they never officially dated or were married to that woman then they weren't ever "involved" with her. If the target finds out down the road that they were having an affair with that particular woman, when confronted, the narcissist might claim that they weren't technically involved and because the target wasn't clear, they told them what they felt to be the truth.

With both the plausible denial as well as their redefining words on the fly, the target eventually realizes that they can never fully tell what's happening. You may find yourself asking them the same question, worded in ten different ways, just to make sure you've covered all your bases, and then you still wonder what you've missed and how you can be clearer with your communication. And frankly, it doesn't matter how clear and direct you are, because if they can't play the semantic shuffle or redefine reality, they will most likely resort to either blaming you or someone else, or just flat-out lie about what they did. So don't be fooled into thinking that the issue is with your communication, if the tables were turned, and you were to play the semantic shuffle or redefining reality game with them, they'd be outraged.

Incoherent mumbling. They will mumble something incoherently in the middle of a discussion, but won't repeat it when asked, and will often accuse the target of not listening to them. Then, if the issue comes up later, they will say, "I TOLD you ..." This seems to be a type of "insurance" for them. It is a way for them to avoid being accountable, because however things turn out, they can always say, "That's what I said," or, "It's not my fault you didn't hear me."

Denying their own bad behavior, and instead, bringing up (and focusing on) the target. Because the narcissist is never at fault, and they have a huge sense of entitlement to do whatever they please, they believe that their behavior should never be in question; instead, any potential problem that someone else has with their behavior is invalid, and the focus quickly shifts to make the target the problem, and the conversation is derailed.

Example:

Target: "Why is that woman texting you sexy pictures of herself?"

Narcissist: Well, you still talk to your ex-husband."

Target: "What does that have to do with anything? I only talk to my ex when I have to–and even then, we only talk about the kids."

Narcissist: "Well, I don't like that you talk to him, but I don't say anything to you about that. I think you still want him back. I mean, how do I really know I can trust you? You could be cheating on me with him for all I know."

Narcissistic Abuse: This is a term that originated in the early twentieth century due in large part to the work by famed psychologist, Alice Miller. Miller used the term "narcissistic abuse" to refer to a specific type of emotional abuse against children that resulted from narcissistic parents who required their child to give up their own wants, needs, and feelings, (i.e.; their individuality) in order to meet the parent's needs for self-esteem. In this dynamic, the narcissistic parent only saw the child as an extension of themselves and not the child for who they were.

The term "narcissistic abuse" has since grown to include any type of dynamic with a narcissistic person in which the abuser seeks to get their needs and wants met at the expense of another. The way a narcissist goes about getting others to give up their wants, needs, and feelings and to try to be what the narcissist wants them to be is through using, abusing, and exploiting them. There are seven main types of abuse (verbal, emotional, psychological, sexual, financial, spiritual, physical), and one or more forms of abusive behavior are used in order to get the target under the narcissist's control so they can be used to meet their wants and needs.

However, while the term narcissistic abuse applies to any dynamic in which a person is being used, abused, exploited, or neglected to meet the needs and wants of a narcissistic person, many people tend to use the term narcissistic abuse to mainly refer to more covert forms of verbal, emotional, and psychological abuse, such as gaslighting, subtle jabs and put downs, and the slow and systematic grinding down of a person's self-esteem and self-image. In other words, it's often used to describe the more psychological (or "invisible") aspects of abuse, as any form of abuse that doesn't leave physical bruises is often minimized and seen by many as "not really abuse" because there are no visible signs of abuse, violence, or harm.

But make no mistake, the psychological and emotional damage that is done often causes long-lasting emotional and physical damage. A person who goes through narcissistic abuse is often left not knowing who they are, not knowing how they feel, not trusting their judgment, and not knowing the difference between safe and dangerous behavior. They often find themselves in a series of narcissistic relationships, friendships, and other abusive dynamics. This is in large part due to the manipulative nature of narcissists who continue to use, abuse, and exploit their targets, and deny, minimize, or blame their target for the abuse. Narcissists often have a careless and cruel indifference about the damage their behavior causes, a jaw-dropping level of entitlement, a lack of sincere remorse (or a lack of remorse at all), and never-ending justifications for their abuse. Over time, this damaging, destructive, and sometimes even deadly behavior, and the target's justifications of it become the target's new normal. And the target quickly learns that the narcissist's "love" is conditional. Either the target conforms to the narcissist's every whim and expectation, or any crumbs of attention and affection that they give them will be withheld. As any relationship with a narcissist is a one-sided relationship, with everything being all about the narcissist doing whatever they want to do, and in the narcissist's mind, anyone who has a problem with that is crazy, difficult, too sensitive, cruel, manipulative, and abusive to them!

*In the following examples, I focus mainly on the dynamics between parents and children, as the other examples in this book are primarily about dating or marital relationships.

Here are some examples of narcissistic abuse in motion:

- A parent who continually "taunts and teases" (psychologically abuses) a child about their appearance or choices and then when the child cries, or the parent tells them to stop, they blame the child for being too sensitive or too emotional.

- A parent who either makes their child sick, continually insists that their child is sick (when the child isn't) or exaggerates their symptoms because the parent likes getting the attention and sympathy from others due to their sick, dying, or dead child. (This is also known as Munchausen by proxy.)

- A parent who expects their child to act like an adult and places their responsibility onto the child, turning the child into either the primary or secondary caregiver of either the parent or of the other children. This might be a mother whose husband has left and now she expects her ten-year old son to act like the man of the house, to cook her dinner, listen to her vent about anything and everything, and forgo spending time with his friends. He is made to feel guilty for ever wanting to pursue his own wants and needs, or for having any problem with taking care of her emotionally, physically, and when he's older, financially.

- A spouse who continually lies and cheats but continues to keep their spouse in the marriage with false promises of change because they like having two incomes, as well as having their spouse cook and clean for them.

- A parent who uses guilt, shame, and sympathy to get their adult child to continually give them money—even if it's destroying their adult child's marriage or putting the adult child in a financial bind.

- A parent who insists that their adult child work in their family business but then pays them significantly less than the fair market value for their work, and makes their child feel guilty, greedy, and ungrateful for wanting to get paid more.

- A spouse who makes their partner feel lazy, selfish, and bad for being sick in bed with the flu, and unable to make them and their needs (cooking dinner, having sex, etc.) a priority.

- A parent who doesn't spend any money on a child's basic needs such as clothes that fit, taking them to the doctor or to the dentist, but then the parent spending their money on extras such as getting their nails and hair done, or buying an expensive new car.

- A spouse who is overly critical and undermining of the other spouse by continually telling them all the reasons that whatever they want to do will not work. They might say things such as, "No one would hire you," or "You are too old to go back to school—besides, I don't think you're smart enough anyway." If the spouse tries to defend their decision, the narcissist will most likely claim that they are just being honest, and that it's the target's fault for not being able to handle the truth.

- A parent who locks their child (who has a fear of the dark) in a dark basement for an hour as punishment for something. When the child is released from the basement and starts to cry, the parent gets annoyed and upset with the child for crying, and blames the child for what happened telling them that they wouldn't have acted that way if they had just listened or if they weren't so difficult—and that they should be grateful that they don't hit them or beat them with a belt like some other parent might do.

\-   A spouse who baits their partner into a fight by planting seeds of jealousy and insecurity and then when the spouse questions them about it or gets upset, they spin it and exclaim that the spouse is crazy and overly emotional.

\-   A parent who lies, abuses, and steals from their child, but if the child tries to protest or cut off contact, they use guilt, obligation, and twisted views of religion (spiritual abuse) to keep them around, claiming that they need to honor their parents, and that they need to forgive and forget.

\-   A person who seeks out single parents on dating sites in order to lure them by pretending to be a loving and caring partner, all so that they can molest their children once trust is established.

\-   A parent who uses guilt, shame, and obligation in order to manipulate a child from asking for basic (and reasonable) requests such as food, hygiene needs, medical or dental care, money to buy a gift for a friend's birthday present, or clothes that fit properly. If the child protests, the parent may spin things around and tell the child that they are the ones who are greedy, demanding, insensitive, uncaring, selfish, and manipulative.

\-   A person who is manipulative and abusive towards their partner and who then accuses their partner of being the one who is manipulative and abusive.

\-   A spiritual leader or therapist who takes great pride (and gets their self-esteem needs met) in their ability to keep marriages together…even if these marriages are abusive.

- A parent who steals their child's identity and opens up credit cards in their name.

- A parent who has their child's life planned out for them, including what kind of hobbies they will (or won't) have, where they will go to college, or what profession they should have. For example, a parent who insists that their child give up their love of art and instead become a doctor. Or a parent who insists that their young child take up acting or modeling because they were either an actress or a model, or because they never got to be an actress or a model and are trying to live out their dream through their child. And if the child doesn't want to do these things, they are often told that they are ungrateful, spoiled, bratty, difficult, having a bad attitude and will never amount to anything.

Narcissistic Abuse (Symptoms): During and after an abusive relationship, a person often feels a major shift in their personality.

The symptoms of abuse include:

- Wanting to avoid other people.

- Feeling distrustful of others.

- Having a loss of interest in things that were once enjoyable.

- Having no desire to date (this can go on for years after the relationship ends).

- Having a lack of desire and fear to ever be emotionally vulnerable to anyone.

- Feeling detached or numb, feeling hopeless about the future.

- Having sleeping or eating difficulties.

- Being irritable.

- Being easily startled.

- Feeling hyper-vigilant.

- Having flashbacks of abusive things that were said and done.

- Feeling hopeless.

- Feeling like their life is a movie and not something that's really happening to them.

- Developing psychosomatic illnesses (pain with no physical cause).

- Fatigue, feeling overwhelmed by small, everyday tasks.

- Loss of self-esteem.

- Feeling alone in their pain.

- Being depressed.

- Engaging in self-harming behaviors such as drinking, drug use, or cutting.

- Thoughts of suicide.

- Feeling at fault for the abuse.

- Panic attacks.

- Rage at the abuser, or even feeling suicidal or homicidal.

It's also very common for targets of narcissistic abuse to feel embarrassment and shame and to blame themselves for what happened (in part because they were blamed for the abuse and also because they feel ashamed for not seeing the abusive behavior for what it was sooner, and for not leaving sooner).

After leaving the relationship, many targets often need constant reassurance of decisions they are making or of their thought processes in general because they have experienced gaslighting and other manipulative techniques designed to erode their sanity. Even if the relationship did not contain gas lighting, or any forms of overt abuse, seeing the narcissist's "mask slip," and realizing they had been used, abused, and exploited for the narcissists own selfish reasons, is enough to shatter a person's concept of what is real, and who can be trusted. This is often the case with people who find out that their seemingly ideal partner was living a double life, and was only using them for sex, money, social status, or for some other reason.

In addition, many abuse targets develop Stockholm syndrome and want to support, defend, and love their abuser despite what they have gone endured. This is why many targets in response to the question, of "Why didn't you leave?" will answer, "Because I loved them," or "Because they were my mom/dad/child/friend/etc." To the outside world, this explanation doesn't seem to make any sense, because being used, abused, and exploited isn't love, but to the person who was in this dynamic, they were conditioned to think that how they were treated wasn't a problem, it was partially their fault, or that it was somehow part of the normal highs and lows of a relationship. In addition, to the person who got caught up in this "manipulationship" —they had real feelings involved, and real attachments were made and sorting out what happened and how they feel takes time. Because an abusive relationship is, at the core, a confusing relationship.

Example: Sally was recently discarded on her birthday by Jace, her boyfriend of ten months. Two days after he broke up with her, he began posting pictures of him and his new girlfriend on Facebook, and about how happy they were. Sally was devastated, and couldn't believe he could move on so fast. It was like she and their relationship meant nothing.

During the time they were together, Sally felt like she was on an emotional roller coaster. The good times with Jace were really good and made her feel like he was her soul mate, but the bad times were really bad and included cheating, lying, and lots of yelling, name calling, put downs, and criticism. Although the bad times were really bad, she'd held onto hope that if she could just get through to him to let him know how hurtful his behavior was that eventually he'd stop.

Now that the relationship ended, she's had a hard time falling asleep, and when she does she either has nightmares or very emotional dreams about him, and wakes up screaming or crying. She often feels numb or full of rage, and only leaves the house to go to work or to get groceries. She finds herself thinking about him all the time and rehashing both the good and bad times. Family and friends tell her that he was a loser and that she should be glad he's gone, and while on one level she knows that is true, she can't help but be concerned that maybe the way he treated her was partially her fault. She wonders if she'd only been more careful about how she brought up issues she had with their relationship that maybe he wouldn't have yelled so much or called her names…and maybe he wouldn't have left. She finds herself obsessively looking at his Facebook page and thinking about him all the time.

In many ways, she feels addicted to him, and a part of her hopes that maybe he'll contact her. At one point she breaks down and texts him, telling him that she misses him, and he sends her a text back with a picture of him and his new girlfriend in bed together, and tells her to stop stalking him, and that she is pathetic, crazy, and needs therapy. Sally is crushed. She wonders if perhaps she really was the problem. And perhaps most devastatingly of all, she fears that maybe she lost her soul mate, and that she'll never experience that kind of intense soul mate type of connection again.

(I'm going to continue this example, as I think it's important to address what happens to many people when they seek help from professionals who are not familiar with "narcissistic abuse" (emotional and psychological abuse).

After months of being on an intense emotional roller coaster and struggling with depression, anxiety, bouts of rage, and feeling like her life and her sense of self are blown apart, she decides to see a psychiatrist. When she does, the psychiatrist diagnoses her with having Borderline Personality Disorder because she has a fragmented sense of self, intense emotions, often feels suicidal, and has a pattern of unstable relationships. Sally goes home and begins to research both disorders, and much to her horror, she finds out online that Borderline Personality Disordered people are often abusive and manipulative—and can be just as problematic as narcissists. She is devastated and suicidal, as these diagnoses are now confirmation to her that she was the problem all along. Her psychiatrist has a therapist in his office that he recommends she start seeing. She tells her therapist about her last relationship, and the therapist tells her that every relationship takes two people to make it work and asks her about her part in things. Sally feels like she is being blamed for Jace's behavior, and with her new diagnosis, she is more confused than ever.

She decides to join a support group for Borderline Personality Disorder. She begins to open up about her devastation about her diagnoses and how her behavior chased off her soul mate. The more details she gave about her last relationship, the more it became clear to other members in the group that she was in an abusive relationship, and is seeing two professionals who don't understand the dynamics (or aftermath) of an abusive relationship. Sally realizes her relationship wasn't perfect, but since she was never hit, she doesn't feel comfortable calling it abusive. The more she learns about verbal, emotional, and psychological abuse, and the more she hears stories from others, the more her behavior makes sense. Some of these members began telling her that trauma and PTSD from abuse are commonly misdiagnosed as Borderline Personality Disorder, and encourage her to see a therapist who specializes in trauma. Again, Sally feels like she was overreacting by referring to her relationship with Jace as "trauma," as it wasn't like he beat her. Members of the group explained that all abusive behavior causes some degree of trauma, and that a person doesn't need to go through the worst of the worst in order to become traumatized or to develop PTSD. The members also reassure her that the problems in her relationship weren't communication issues; they were power and control issues—and they were

Jace's issues, not hers. They encourage her to explore the topics of healthy boundaries and deal breakers, as well as the different forms of abuse—and how abusive people go about eroding a person's boundaries and then grinding down their sense of self-worth and making them think they deserve the abuse.

Many members also tell her that they were misdiagnosed with the same disorders and felt even more depressed and suicidal. They told her that even if she did have Borderline Personality, that this didn't necessarily make her abusive. They encouraged her to ask herself if she had these kinds of behaviors (or felt this way) before this relationship, or if she began feeling this way after this relationship. Sally realized that she'd never had issues like this before, decided to join a support group for abuse, as well as to seek out a therapist who specialized in abuse and EFT or EMDR treatments for trauma, and to get a second opinion from that therapist about her previous diagnosis.

Once Sally began to get treatment for her PTSD and began reading more about abusive behavior, it was like the pieces of the puzzle clicked into place, and she began to move forward in her healing.

Narcissistic Injury: This is a real or perceived threat to a narcissist's ego which usually results with them going into attack mode, known as "narcissistic rage." This attack mode can happen subtly and behind the scenes, or it can happen with them exploding and going on a verbal and/or physical attack. A narcissistic injury could happen in any number of ways, but perhaps the most common are challenging the narcissist's decisions or abilities, critiquing them, questioning them about their problematic behavior, setting boundaries, talking positive-ly about others, talking positively about good things in your life or even talking about positive things in the life of their children or other family members.

Everyone gets jealous or envious of others from time-to-time, and no one really likes feeling challenged or questioned—and this is all normal to an extent. What's not normal is to fly off the handle or to have a meltdown when things don't go our way. However, with narcissists, they have a paper-thin ego, and any criticism to them or something good that is happening to someone else is perceived as an attack. Because narcissists go into attack mode when their ego is threatened or when they start to lose power over their target, a target of abuse needs to be careful when they go about leaving them, as this is when they are the most dangerous. It is always a good idea to anticipate how you think they might respond, and then to err on the side of caution. Even if a narcissist has never been physically violent before, they can easily become violent during this time.

Example: Julio tells his work buddy Todd that he is excited about his new promotion. As he talks about how he's so relieved to be able to pay off some debt with the money from his pay raise, Julio notices a sneer briefly flash across Todd's face. This strikes him as odd since they are friends and work in different departments—it's not like Julio got the promotion over Todd. Soon after Julio had told Todd about his promotion, Todd's behavior radically changed. He became cold and critical of Julio and began making snide comments about his choice in clothing, his weight, and how easy his job was compared to Todd's. He would say things like, "Now that you've got some extra money, maybe you can get a tie that's not from the 1980's," or once when Todd passed his office, he made a comment about how Julio's pizza smelled good, but that he worked too hard at the gym and didn't want to let himself become fat. During this time, Julio began noticing that faxes from his clients began to go missing. The first few times this happened, he chalked it up to the fax machine being on the fritz. It wasn't until paperwork began to go missing from his office that he began to wonder if he was going crazy. Still thinking that Todd was his friend, he mentioned this to him, and Todd told him that maybe he was under too much stress with his new promotion. Julio began to wonder if Todd was right.

About a week later, Julio overheard Todd telling their supervisor that Julio was very unprofessional with clients and had also been making a lot of mistakes at work—and that he was concerned about him. Maybe he had a drinking problem, as Julio had always been such a great employee. None of this was true, and Julio then realized that Todd wasn't his friend, and was in fact out to get him fired. He also began to wonder if Todd was responsible for all of his missing paperwork. Julio realized he needed to distance himself from Todd, as well as talk to his supervisor in order to let him know what has been happening.

Example: Linda always felt as though her mother was in competition with her when it came to men. Linda's mother has always dressed overly sexy and acted immature and flirtatious around men. She always had to be the center of attention, and growing up, Linda had dreaded her mother showing up to her school for any event or parent-teacher conference.

Linda recently began dating, and her boyfriend had made the comment on Facebook that Linda was "the most beautiful girl in the world." When Linda's mother read this comment, she flew into a rage, accusing Linda of being a whore, and demanding that she stop seeing him. When Linda protested, her mother began yelling at her, calling her names and belittling her.

Example: When Jane's verbally abusive husband, Ryan, came home from work, she told him she was filing for divorce. Ryan flew into a rage and began yelling, cussing at her, and calling her names. Ryan threw her keys at her and told her to get the hell out of his house, and she had better watch her back.

Example of projection and a perceived narcissistic injury: Sam and Karen had been dating for five months, and up until recently things had been great. Over the past few weeks, Sam began accusing Karen of cheating on him. Karen was shocked by these accusations as she wasn't cheating and was confused as to why he'd even think that. He began insisting that she didn't wear makeup and for her to stop going to the gym, because he accused her of trying to make herself attractive to other men. He began texting her often during the day and would become upset when she couldn't text him back right away and began accusing her of being too busy having sex with her coworkers. He began going through her laundry and insisting he smelled cologne on her clothes. What Karen thought was so strange was that Sam had quite a few women texting him and sending him sexy pictures, and if anyone was cheating, it was most likely him. No matter how much she altered her behavior to try to convince Sam that she wasn't cheating on him, nothing seemed to help, and his behavior was getting worse with time, not better. Karen knew she should probably break up with him, but she was scared to do so, as she knew he'd think she was leaving him for another man—even though she wasn't.

(Sam was most likely cheating on Karen, projecting his behavior onto her, and then lashing out at her for what he was in fact doing. And if Karen were to point out to him that he is most likely projecting, in an attempt to give him some insight as to his behavior, Sam would likely become enraged. Because when a person is projecting their "uncomfortable" or bad thoughts, feelings, and actions onto others, they are doing so in attempt to distance themselves from what they are doing. In other words, if a person can't handle the truth about their behavior, and then they are confronted with that truth—especially by their target/scapegoat—this will most likely only make their defenses escalate, and the abuse becomes worse.)

Example: Scott recently broke up with his girlfriend Kim. He couldn't handle anymore of her "psycho" behavior and controlling ways. Ten minutes later she began sending him a barrage of texts calling him names and threatening to tell everyone that he had raped her if he didn't respond. Scott became enraged and scared that she would accuse him of raping her, but still he knew he needed not to respond. His friends told him to make sure to keep all the texts from her, in case he did wind up in court, and to block her number, which he did. Later on that night Kim showed up at his house, screaming out on his front lawn, demanding that he talk to her. He immediately called the police, and when they got there, they told her to leave—which she did. As he was leaving work that next week, he discovered that his car had been keyed.

Example: Karen and Chuck dated for a few months when she began to notice that he seemed to have a lot of female friends. When she asked him about this, he responded that he remained friends with many of his exes, and that he also got along better with women in general. Karen wasn't really comfortable with this, and as more time went on, she became more uncomfortable because these women texted him often and many sent him sexy pictures. When she expressed her concern, he flew into a rage and began accusing her of being jealous, insecure, and controlling. Karen was shocked at his response and told him that they needed to break up. Chuck continued with his rant saying that she should be so lucky to date a man like him, and that he was the best she'd ever get. Karen didn't take his insults personally. She took them as conformation that he had major issues and was not the kind of guy she'd ever want to date. She knew from past experience that people like Chuck don't tend to go away easily or quietly, and in an attempt to limit any drama that he might attempt to start up again, she blocked his number and blocked him on all social media.

Narcissist: In a nutshell, narcissists are people whose actions are entirely self-centered and self-serving, to the point that their behavior causes major disruption in their lives and trauma to the lives of those closest to them (whether they realize it or not). They are often charismatic, convincing, and can be very charming when they want (or need) to be. They have a need for admiration, and are often very focused on impressing others and maintaining their public image. They tend to feel entitled to treat others however they wish, and because of this they have a lack of empathy, regard, and remorse for the results of their actions.

In short, they feel that they should be able to do whatever they want, whenever they want, as much as they want, and with whomever they want, and anyone that disagrees with them is the problem (and the enemy).

It's important to realize that there is something called "healthy narcissism" because I see a lot of targets of abuse get concerned that they might be a narcissist if they make their wants, needs, or feelings a priority. This is generally because they've often been told by a narcissist that anything that they wanted, needed, or felt was bad, wrong, selfish, manipulative, or abusive. They may struggle with feeling like a narcissist if they set boundaries, have deal breakers, and don't put everyone else's needs, wants, and feelings ahead of their own.

Healthy narcissism is a term that refers to a level of healthy and realistic level of self-esteem. A person who has a healthy level of narcissism believes that their wants, needs, and feelings are just as important as anyone else's and feels worthy of making themselves a priority.

They have a realistic sense of themselves and their abilities which is in alignment with reality. They usually set realistic goals for themselves, but even if their goals are higher than their current abilities, they also realize that in order to achieve those goals they are going to have to work hard and learn new skills to achieve them.

One last point about narcissists: many people take issue with the word "narcissist" and feel it should only be used to describe those who have been officially diagnosed with Narcissistic Personality Disorder. There are many problems with this view. First, the vast majority of narcissists won't go to a therapist (and therefore they don't get diagnosed). If they do go to a therapist, they can often charm the therapist into thinking they don't have a problem. They may even convince the therapist that their target is the one with the problem. What's important is to realize that the terms "narcissist" and "narcissistic behavior" both point to highly problematic behavior. A person who has persistently entitled, abusive, or exploitative behavior regardless of what you call them or their behavior; it's still a problem. Because narcissists (and their behavior) come across in different ways, this next section covers some different subtypes of narcissists and how their behavior tends to manifest itself.

Covert Narcissist (or Vulnerable Narcissist): Vulnerable narcissists are also self-absorbed, self-centered, and have a lack of empathy and remorse. Where they differ from a more textbook narcissist (often called a "grandiose" narcissist) is that vulnerable narcissists tend to show more emotional depth (when they are wounded) and are very concerned with how others see them. They are thought to fear abandonment and perceive any type of mistake, criticism, rejection, or "inferior" treatment by others as such. They think of themselves as superior beings and often crumble when others don't think the same. This crumbling reveals their vulnerability and often comes across as their appearing as a deeply-wounded child. Their inflated sense of self-worth and need to be acknowledged as important and superior is most likely a compensation for their low self-esteem. And their fear of abandonment is thought to be a result due to a lack of secure bonding with their parents when they were a child.

When a vulnerable narcissist's wounding is visible, it can really pull at a person's heartstrings. The target may watch with amazement as the narcissist emotionally transforms into a small child. They may cry, stay in bed, fall into a depression, or need a seemingly large amount of reassurance that they are okay or that they did a good job. And a target of a vulnerable narcissist may have a hard time distancing themselves from a person like this, because they know how hard they take rejection. They may also think that because the narcissist is capable of being emotionally wounded, that they are capable of empathy and remorse—after all, these narcissists feel emotional pain, so you'd think that they'd be able to sincerely relate to the pain in others (but this is not the case). As soon as they've had enough time to lick their wounds, they are back to their old selfish, insensitive and hurtful, self-absorbed, and entitled ways. Because vulnerable narcissists tend to need reassurance and approval, they also have a hard time being alone. Their partner may have a hard time leaving a vulnerable narcissist because, even despite the abuse they've gone through, they know how fragile the vulnerable narcissist is, and how hard they are going to take the breakup. They may go back if the narcissist threatens to commit suicide or contacts them with repeated pleas for help or to not go.

Covert narcissists often use their vulnerabilities to lure targets in, and to keep them in the cycle of abuse. They may claim that they were abused by their ex, or by a parent—and that they are afraid to be hurt again. Or they may build up their target by telling them how wonderful, attractive, and special they are. The target may find themselves continually reassuring them that they are also wonderful, attractive, and special and that they would never hurt them.

Example: Tina met Roger online. She really liked that he was a teacher and worked with children. Roger was kind, compassionate, and very attentive...but seemingly very insecure. He would tell Tina that he'd never dated anyone like her before and that he was incredibly lucky that she was interested in him. Tina was flattered that he thought so highly of her, and would continually reassure him that she thought he was a great catch too. Everything was great for the first few weeks, and then Susan noticed that Roger would say things about other women that she found odd. He began telling her about a coworker who dressed sexy and how he found it distracting. At first Tina wondered why he was telling her this, but she brushed it off. Then a week or so later, he told her that a woman bought him a drink when he was out with friends because she liked his beard. Again, Tina thought this was odd, but this time she asked him why he accepted the drink when they were dating. At this, Roger flew into a rage and began yelling at her, accusing her of being jealous and controlling, and then gave her the silent treatment for a week. Tina was confused and devastated. When Roger reopened communication with her, she was relieved, and she apologized. Things went back to being great, and then a few weeks later, Roger's "Mr. Hyde" side came out, and he began verbally abusing her after she told him she wasn't staying the night because she didn't feel well.

Example: Trevor and his girlfriend Diane went downtown for a big New Year's Eve party. When they got back to their hotel, Trevor realized he'd lost his cell phone and began to cry really hard. At first, Diane thought he was joking because his reaction was so disproportionate to the situation, especially since he was normally somewhat of an arrogant tough guy. When she realized he was serious, she tried to comfort him. She told him that she was sorry this happened, and shared a time when she lost her phone. She went on to say that the good news was that he had insurance on it, and they could get a new one tomorrow. Diane tried to reassure him that these things sometimes happen, and that it wasn't his fault, but Trevor wouldn't hear it. He told her that these things didn't happen to him, and he couldn't believe how stupid he was. He curled up under the covers for the rest of the night and refused any of Diane's attempts to console him. Diane was really caught off guard by his behavior, as here was this tough, adult man who seemed to have changed into a small child. She had never seen Trevor, or any adult, act like this before.

Overt Narcissist (or Grandiose Narcissist): This type of narcissist is more obvious, and tends to be a textbook example of what most people expect a narcissist to be. Overt narcissists are usually grandiose, arrogant, overly-confident and self-assured, obnoxious, and charismatic. They do not seek approval, fear rejection, or show emotion like vulnerable narcissists do. If they are rejected or insulted, they don't crumble like a vulnerable narcissist does—instead they go on the attack, and they don't stop until they've sufficiently ground down their "opponent" for not treating them with the admiration and respect they feel they so rightfully deserve. Grandiose narcissists don't need the support and reassurance of others like vulnerable narcissists do. It's thought that grandiose narcissists aren't compensating for a lack of self-esteem, but more so that their inflated sense of self comes from being spoiled and/or their parents telling them how special, amazing, and talented they were, without balancing that with proper discipline and a more realistic view of themselves and their shortcomings.

All overt narcissists are delusional and grandiose to some extent; however, some are delusional to an extreme. Those at the far end of the spectrum tend to think they have special abilities or powers such as the ability to time travel, that they are a prophet or God, the reincarnation of deity or of a famous person from history, a direct connection to extra-terrestrials, the salvation of the human race, or have extra-sensory abilities or powers. They may even claim to have been subjected to persecution of some sort due to their special status and powers (such as kidnapping, torture, alien abduction, or ritualistic cult abuse), although they are unable to prove any of these claims. Cult leaders would fall under this category. Most delusional narcissists tend to be overt narcissists, but many can have covert features as well—crumbling emotionally and needing a lot of reassurance if their delusions are questioned or are not taken seriously by others.

Example: Charlotte's popularity in certain "spiritual" and supernatural circles was growing. She was intelligent, beautiful, and very convincing. A large part of her appeal was that she claimed to be a psychic, as well as to have a host of other super-natural abilities such as teleportation, clairaudience, and clairsentience. She had other grandiose and delusional claims, such as stating she was the reincarnation of Cleopatra and had been the target of government programs and a satanic cult due to her superhuman powers—none of which could be proven. She had thousands of followers who had turned over large sums of money to help support her spiritual mission of cleaning their energetic vibrations so that their souls could travel back to the star system from which they all originated.

Example: Jerry, the top-selling agent in a real-estate firm, had married the office secretary, Tina close to ten years ago. When Tina first met Jerry, she was drawn to how confident, outgoing, and self-assured he was. However, many other people (including most of his coworkers) thought Jerry was an arrogant, pompous, obnoxious jerk who was difficult to be around for any length of time. These ten years have been an emotional roller coaster, with Jerry's cheating, alcohol, and poor money management peppered with promises of change that never lasted for long. However, in Tina's mind, she took a certain degree in comfort in thinking that Jerry would always stay with her, as they'd gone through so much together (when really he'd put her through so much). When Tina developed cancer, Jerry told her he couldn't handle the stress, and he moved out. Tina then realized that her relationship with Jerry would forever be one-sided, and that he did not have the emotional capacity or desire to care for her or her needs.

Altruistic Narcissist: This is a type of narcissist who gets their ego stroked from appearing kind, good, and caring, but they only do so in order to get the praise and validation that comes from being seen as a good and caring person. Everything they do is for show. They often give money they don't have and gifts they can't afford. And if their charitable acts are denied, they often become angry and enraged. Altruistic narcissists may volunteer a lot, be leaders of a spiritual group, or work in a position that is seen as caring (such as a teacher, nurse, doctor, counselor, social worker, director of a non-profit, etc.). However, those who know them best, realize that there are always strings attached to their acts of kindness and that they are better off not receiving any help from them. These acts of kindness are either held over their head and expected to be repaid ten-fold, or they are used to lure people in so they can be exploited. The behavior of an altruistic narcissist tends to come across as confusing, because on one hand the narcissist is so charitable and considerate, and seems to care so deeply, but their emotions seem shallow and insincere and their actions seem like they are for show…because they are.

Example: For the past three years in a row, Susan has won the company award for the most volunteer hours given to their designated charity. At every event, Susan makes sure to take lots of pictures of herself helping and posts them all over her various social media accounts. She places volunteering and the needs of strangers over the needs of her children and husband. Her children and husband are resentful at how much time she spends helping others and all the accolades she gets, while at home she is either cruel and calloused or simply emotionally unavailable. She'd rather be seen as kind and compassionate by total strangers, than by loving towards, or loved by, her family.

Example: James is a handsome and charismatic pastor of a local church, who is married with two adult children, and several foster children—which his wife cares for, while he gets all the credit. He has the kind of personality where men admire him, and women adore him. He shovels snow during the winter for elderly parishioners, plays Santa during Christmas, volunteers at the local food bank, and builds houses for the poor. His adult children have struggled with what to think of their father, as on one hand he seems so loving and compassionate to others, but has been emotionally (and physically) unavailable, hurtful, and cruel to both them and their mother. Over the years, they've grown tired of hearing about how their father is such a wonderful man, when behind closed doors he is very different.

Cerebral Narcissist: Cerebral narcissists take great pride in their intellect and are often extremely intelligent and convincing. What makes them different from an intellectual person who enjoys a good discussion, or who enjoys teaching others, is that a cerebral narcissist leverages their intelligence in order to "win." They often proclaim that they are logical and reasonable—even though their opinions and arguments are often anything but. Because they often come across with such great conviction, they can say the most outlandish, hateful, or dangerous things and spin it in such a way that they come across as balanced and fair.

They are usually incredibly persuasive, intelligent, quick-witted, and able to shift between logic, logical fallacies, lies, name calling, and anger to knock their "opponent" off balance, as well as to make their point. They often have advanced degrees or high levels of success (or claim to), and to those who see through them, come across as pretentious, grandiose, and exhausting. They rarely like to associate with anyone below their (perceived or even fabricated) intellect, educational or financial level, and when they do so, it's generally in order to engage them in some sort of argument so that they can win.

What can be so crazy-making is that these narcissists continually shift their argument and use a series of logical fallacies, reductionist arguments, lies, half-truths, word salad, and semantic ploys to frustrate and exhaust the other person until that person becomes exhausted or explodes in anger, at which point the narcissist will declare that the other person is too unreasonable, illogical, or too emotional. It's like the saying goes, arguing with a narcissist is like playing chess with a pigeon. No matter how good you are, the pigeon is going to knock over all the pieces, poop on the board and act victorious.

Example: Doug considers himself a genius, comparing himself to the character "Sheldon" on the TV show, "The Big Bang Theory" and often talks about how lonely it is for him not to be able to find friends or girlfriends who are on par with his intellect. He doesn't often date, and when he does, the relationships start to crumble as soon as his girlfriend's begin to challenge him or assert their own opinions. Whenever this happens, Doug flies into a rage and either begins yelling, belittling them, or he gives them the silent treatment. The same pattern has happened with his friends, as many of his former friends' wives refused to have Doug around as he would continually try to bait them into arguments about their parenting or their role as a wife or mother. Doug's idea of having a conversation was forcing his opinion on others by being what he called "brutally honest" and then making it seem as though they had the issue whenever they got offended by his uninvited (and sexist, racist, and otherwise offensive) "honesty." Doug believed that his views were all based on logic and reason, and that anyone who didn't believe the same was either too emotional or too stupid to see the truth. The real truth was that Doug was a legend in his own mind.

Malignant Narcissist: The term "malignant" means dangerous and harmful. A malignant narcissist is one who has all the traits of a narcissist (grandiosity, seeks approval and attention, lacks empathy, lacks remorse, entitlement, and fragile self-esteem) as well as a blend of Antisocial Personality Disorder traits such as charm, aggression, a lack of regard for rules or laws, paranoia, and, in addition, is often sadistic. Their level of superiority far surpasses being arrogant, obnoxious, and self-centered, and is often dangerous, destructive, and deadly. Even though they need approval and attention of others (unlike a psychopath), they still view others as expendable and feel justified by harming them. For those who have experienced this type of person, they often report feeling a "dark" energy about them, fearful or terrified of what they might do—even though they might not have done or said anything overtly that they can point to as the reason they feel this way.

Example: Diane met George on a dating website, and before

long the two were inseparable. Diane felt like she'd won the relationship lottery and felt as though she'd met her soul mate. No man had ever been so good to her. George would bring her coffee in bed every morning and cook dinner at night. All of his actions made her feel incredibly special and loved. Everyone seemed to really like George, except her mother, who pulled her aside and told her that she felt like something was very off about him, but that she couldn't put her finger on it. Diane brushed off her mother's concerns being due to how fast they were moving, which Diane knew was probably too fast, but everything just felt so right. They were married within a few months of knowing each other, and a few months later they'd opened up a business—all of which Diane financed. Six months into the business, George had convinced Diane to add his name to everything, including her house they also took out life insurance policies on each other.

It was around this time that a series of bizarre and dangerous events began to occur. Within a period of three months, she was the victim of two hit-and-run accidents and a botched home invasion. People began to joke about how lucky she was, and at one point her best friend joked that perhaps George was trying to kill her. Up until that moment Diane hadn't even thought that could be a possibility, but now she was starting to wonder. The final straw was when the insurance company had called her to let her know that George had raised the amount on her insurance policy to over a million dollars, and that it was company policy to let a person know. Diane moved out that afternoon while George was away and immediately filed for divorce. George flew into a rage when he saw her at the courthouse and told her that he didn't need her smearing his name all over town. Diane was shocked at how quickly George seemed to go from loving her to hating her. Shortly after their divorce, Diane found a tremendous amount of debt that George had racked up that she never knew about, along with numerous charges to an escort service. Diane couldn't believe what a nightmare her Prince Charming turned out to be.

Somatic Narcissist: Somatic narcissists get their ego fed mainly through their attractiveness, power, money, or sex. They are often shallow and associate with either other shallow people, or those who have power and money. They tend to be hyper-sexual, focused on their physical appearance, and are often very status-driven. They are often very seductive, and are usually pathological cheaters. They may be highly successful or they may latch onto others and use them for social status or money. Sex is their main weapon, and they can put on a great performance in bed, becoming the most amazing sexual partner their target has ever had, and using their seduction and sexual prowess to create what feels like a real soul mate connection.

Example: Rachel met James at a local café and soon after, their relationship picked up speed. Rachel had never experienced the kind of chemistry and passion she felt with James, and the sex was off-the-charts. Soon after, James moved in with her, and claimed to have been fired from his job. Rachel was understanding…for the first few months, but then began to grow resentful that she was paying all of the bills. James said that he was looking for a job, but that everything was way below his skill level. It was around this time that Rachel began to notice that James seemed to have a lot of female friends—most of whom he seemed to be secretive about. Whenever Rachel confronted James about this, or about any of his behavior, he was quick to lose his temper or give her the silent treatment. Their relationship went on like this for over a year, with Rachel feeling torn between feeling like James was a loving, devoted boyfriend who was the best thing that had ever happened to her, or a cheating, lying, mooch who was the worst thing that had ever happened to her. It wasn't until she discovered that he had been siphoning funds out of her account to pay child support to a woman (and a child) she knew nothing about that she decided to leave.

Narcissistic Rage: Narcissistic rage is inappropriate displays of anger from a narcissist that occur on a spectrum ranging from passive-aggressive to aggressive and can be seen as aloofness or cruel indifference (often leading to the silent treatment), irritation or annoyance, to serious outbursts, including verbal and/or physical abuse. Narcissistic rage generally happens after a narcissist receives a "narcissistic injury" or if they perceive that they are losing control over their target or over a situation. On the more mild end of the spectrum, this narcissistic rage can come across as though the narcissist is being immature, bratty, or having an adult temper tantrum. On the more major end of the spectrum, this rage can be terrifying, and they can quickly become violent or deadly.

Example: Jamie caught Todd texting other women...again. She confronted him about it, and he spun it around and began verbally and emotionally abusing her by calling her paranoid, jealous, fat, and worthless, and asking how dare she look at his phone or question him! Todd admitted that he was cheating and blamed Jamie because she was disgusting and had let herself go. After their fight was over and Todd left, Jamie found herself feeling confused about what happened, and wondered if Todd's cheating and his resulting abuse was somehow her fault. Maybe she wasn't home often enough, or maybe she really was all those things that he'd said. After all, she knew she had gained weight over the past year, and she had been concerned he'd been cheating on her for a while. It was all these kernels of truth surrounded in a big ball of a lie that kept her confused and wondering that if she changed, then maybe he'd change too. These seeds of insecurity that Todd's abuse had planted began to erode her self-esteem and her sense of reality. And that was a big part of why she continued to stay with him. She thought she was the problem. And because she was caught up in the cycle of narcissistic abuse, Todd's behavior had just become a new low...and a new normal for their relationship.

Example: Roger recently filed for divorce from his wife Sharon who was verbally and physically abusive. When Sharon got the papers, she flew into a rage, leaving a series of verbally abusive and threatening messages on his voice mail. He hoped that was the end of it, but then later found out she'd called the police on him, filed a protective order against him, and claimed he was abusing her! Her male friends began to harass him at work, and he was concerned that they might gang up on him, or try and make him lose his job. Even though Roger knew what Sharon was saying about him wasn't true, he also realized that most people were probably going to believe her, since he was close to twice her size, and she was a woman. Roger knew she wouldn't handle being served divorce papers well, but he didn't expect her to go this far.

Example: Linda and Thomas had been dating for about six months when she began to see his temper surface on a more regular basis—the latest incident being him raging at her for leaving her dishes in the sink. She'd finally had enough of his anger and called things off with him. He didn't handle it well and began screaming at her on the phone, calling her names and demanding that she talk to him and for her to not hang up on him. She immediately hung up on him and was scared he was going to show up at her door. She finally was able to calm down and go to sleep. When she awoke the next morning, she was shocked to find that Thomas had sent her a barrage of text messages threatening to kill her or whoever else she would date, claiming that she belonged to him and always would.

Narcissistic Smirk: This is a look of smug satisfaction that a narcissist often gets after they've successfully provoked an emotion (jealousy, anger, or fear) in their target that leads to a reaction, or when they otherwise get their way.

Example: Joan wonders if Tony enjoys upsetting her because when they argue, he'll push her buttons until she explodes; then he'll just sit back with this smug little smirk on his face, totally cool, calm, and collected as he tells Joan that she's unstable, has issues, and should really see a therapist for her abusive mistreatment of him and her anger issues.

Dana Morningstar

Narcissistic Supply (or "Supply"): This is a term that is used to describe what feeds a narcissist's ego. Narcissistic supply can be a person, a reaction, attention of any kind, money, power, social status, sex, or admiration.

Example: Jorge was an actor at the local community theater and had a long-standing habit of sleeping his way to the top or as one of his fellow actors sarcastically remarked, "Jorge doesn't just sleep his way to the top, he sleeps his way into getting whatever he wants." To no one's surprise, Jorge's latest boyfriend was the new director and producer of the musical, "West Side Story" where Jorge got the starring role. For those who had known Jorge long enough, the only type Jorge had was someone who had something he wanted. He had his last boyfriend buy him a car, his partner before that to pay off his student loans, and another partner to introduce him to some of the biggest actors in the area.

Example: Jane has had no contact with her ex-boyfriend, John, for six months. Out of the blue, he came back saying he'll give her two months to make things work, and that he's willing to forgive her for everything she's done to him. This text message enrages and confuses Jane, as John was the one who was abusive to her. She really wants to text him that he is a jerk and to remind him of everything he did to her. However, Jane also realizes that John is most likely trying to provoke her into reacting, and she doesn't want to give him the satisfaction of seeing her upset. Instead she decides to block his number and vent about him in her support group instead.

It can be really hard to walk away and say nothing when a person who has wronged you continues to harass and provoke you, but it's important to realize that you can't set them straight, and that by letting them know how hurtful they are, will only feed their ego.

New Supply: A "new supply" is the newest person a narcissist latches onto to drain supply from. This could be a new partner, friend, coworker, etc. Narcissists tend to have a constant source of new supply in their pipeline and move onto their new supply at lightning speed which can be incredibly painful and confusing for those with whom they were previously involved.

Example: Todd met Tina while he was doing an internship overseas. Tina was intelligent, funny, and stunningly beautiful. Their relationship picked up speed fast and within six months they were married. Todd showered Tina with gifts and spent tens of thousands of dollars on clothes, plastic surgery, and a car for her. Todd told Tina that he wouldn't be able to continue spending this kind of money, as he wasn't wealthy—that his money came from an inheritance that was quickly becoming depleted. Within three weeks after this conversation, Tina left, taking everything with her and draining what was left in the account. Todd was devastated, but he was even more devastated when he saw pictures of Tina online with another man.

No Contact: "No contact" means cutting off all contact with a narcissist and not responding to them if they try to reopen contact. For many people, going no contact also means avoiding the narcissist on social media. This may mean blocking them on Facebook or Instagram, or it may mean creating new accounts under a fake name in order to avoid them from sending messages. Going no contact may also involve cutting off contact with friends and family of the narcissist—especially those who are trying to get information about what's going on, or who are trying to push the target back into the relationship.

Going no contact is often the best way to set yourself free from a narcissist because the odds are that they will continue to abuse and use you as long as you let them have access to your life. The only way to get them to leave you alone is to cut off their "supply" of attention that they get from provoking a reaction in you. Often, when a person goes "no contact" with a narcissist, they find that they also need to go no contact with a handful of other people who have become "flying monkeys" and who seek information from them, or who are seeking to abuse, harass, and be rude and hurtful about their relationship. This is because these flying monkeys have been manipulated into thinking the narcissist is the victim and that their target is the manipulative one.

While no contact is seen as the ideal for most people and what many targets of abuse are encouraged to do, this approach may not always be doable or safe. The target may need to formulate a safety plan of escape so that the narcissistic person doesn't fly into a rage once they realize that they are losing power and control over their target and over the situation.

Leaving a narcissist is a lot like kicking a bees' nest. It's a good idea to have a plan in place before you do it. At a minimum, you should err on the side of caution and do what you need to do in order to stay safe and sane, regardless if anyone else agrees with you. There will be no shortage of people who will have a problem with you going no contact. They may think you are selfish, immature, or mean, especially if the abusive person is a family member. Cutting off contact is a healthy and normal response to abusive behavior, and you don't need to justify yourself to anyone.

Example: Bill and Quinn dated for a little over a year. While Bill felt an intense connection and attraction to Quinn, he couldn't stand her controlling, manipulative, and dramatic ways. He had tried to break up with her before, but she'd threaten to commit suicide. She even overdosed on baby Aspirin while they were at a party because she claimed she didn't want to live anymore. Bill suspected she did that because she wanted attention. This last time, when he told her they needed to break up, she then told him she thought she was pregnant with his child. When she said this, Bill saw just how manipulative she was. He realized that if he stayed with her, she would get pregnant on purpose just to trap him. He broke up with her that night and decided to go "no contact." It didn't go over well with Quinn, and over the next few weeks she emailed, called, and texted him hundreds of times, professing her love for him, threatening suicide, and promising to get into therapy. Bill didn't respond. He did however call 911 and told them that she was threatening to kill herself and to please go check on her. He decided to block her phone number, as well as block her on all his social media so she couldn't contact him. He also set up all her emails to go directly to his spam folder. He felt this was the best way to stay no contact as well as to not get upset or sucked back into the relationship.

Example: Rachel was only dating Scott for about two months, but that's all it took for her to recognize that there was something really off about him. Even though she couldn't point to anything specific or majorly wrong in his behavior, there were a bunch of little things e.g. the time he checked out the waitress or the way he badgered her to have sex, even though she told him she wanted to wait. Perhaps the strangest thing was his Facebook profile and how in every picture he looked like a different man. It was like he was a social chameleon and changed into being a different person depending on who he was around.

Rachel had been in an abusive relationship when she was in college, and while that was close to thirty years ago, she found herself having night terrors and feeling that impending sense of doom that she hadn't felt since that relationship in college. She was confused because Scott seemed nothing like Seth, her boyfriend in college, but still she couldn't shake the feeling. She realized over the years that she needed to listen to her gut instincts about people, and since the only other time she felt this way before was with the guy she dated in college, she knew she needed to call things off with Scott. But she also couldn't

166

shake the feeling that Scott could be really dangerous or even deadly. She knew she needed to proceed with caution and not do anything that would send him over the edge. She decided the best approach was to call things off with him in a way that would make everything her fault. That way he wouldn't get upset, and he couldn't argue with her reasons. She called him that night and told him that she'd done a lot of thinking and that she realized she wasn't ready to date anyone. She said that he was an amazing guy, but she just had too many issues. Scott began screaming at her over the phone, calling her names and telling her she was a tease. Rachel realized immediately that she'd made the right decision by ending the relationship. She blocked his number and blocked him on all of her social media accounts. She also went to the store the next day and bought some mace, some motion sensor lights for her house, and a security camera just in case he decided he appeared.

Normalizing: In terms of abuse, normalizing is often a form of justification to excuse problematic behavior, thereby making it somehow normal. People normalize problematic behavior when they are invested in a situation or a person—especially if they have a bond (no matter how toxic) with that person. They may not want to leave because they have an emotional attachment to the person (as with friends, family, or significant others), or they have a physical investment (such as working or going to school overseas and don't want to leave this opportunity because of this abusive person), or a financial investment (they work with this person and can't afford to leave).

The target of abuse may try to convince themselves that the abusive or problematic behavior that they are experiencing is due to the person's childhood, religion, culture, age, gender, appearance, etc. Or they may compare the behavior to abuse they've experienced before, either with this person or with other abusive people from their past and convince themselves that things could be worse.

When a person begins normalizing abusive behavior, they are telling themselves that "this is just how we fight." Normalizing abuse is dangerous because as the abuse escalates (as it generally does), the target continues to lower their standards for how they expect to be treated, to the point where they often feel like a doormat (unable to say no or stand up for themselves, while people walk all over them), or to where harmful/deadly threats or actions by the abuser do not register as harmful or deadly.

Common forms of normalizing problematic behavior are:

-        Thinking that things aren't that bad because the target can still tolerate how they are being treated.

-        Thinking that things are workable because they aren't being hit or aren't being hit that often.

-        Thinking that maybe this time things could be different given enough love, understanding, rehab, therapy, or religion.

Here are some examples of how abusive situations become normalized:

- An abusive person has beaten their partner before, and continues to make death threats such as "Don't play with me," "I'll teach you," or, "They will never find your body" and demands that their target meet them in an empty parking lot, park, or secluded place at night because they want to talk. The target doesn't see anything unsafe or dangerous with meeting them in an isolated place because threats like this are considered a "normal" part of their relationship. Note: This is incredibly dangerous thinking. Never put yourself in a situation that you wouldn't want someone you cared about to endure. (Read that last line a few times and really let it sink it.)

Parental Alienation Syndrome (PAS): This is a term coined by Richard A. Gardner in the early 1980s that describes a significant negative change in a child's behavior toward one parent without justification, where the child becomes belittling and emotionally withdrawn, often to the point where they don't want to spend time with that parent (and sometimes can extend to not wanting to spend time with that parent's family). PAS can be caused intentionally or unintentionally by a child hearing (or overhearing) one parent talking about the other parent in a negative light.

It is important to note that sometimes a parent does need to be alienated, and that contact does need to end for the child's safety. This would be if the parent is dangerous, and if the child is at risk of harm. If this is your situation, talk to an attorney and a therapist well-versed in abusive and manipulative people as well as in PAS about how to handle reducing contact with a destructive or dangerous parent.

Example: Susan and Tom were married for ten years and had a five-year-old son, Peter. When they divorced, Tom would continually tell Peter bad things about his mother. He would tell him that Susan didn't care about Peter because if she did, she wouldn't have divorced him and split up the family. He would also tell Peter he didn't have enough money to buy him toys because he had to pay his mother child support. Peter began to resent his mother for hurting his father and for making it to where he couldn't get any new toys, and started acting out. When Peter would return from visitation, he would act hostile and defiant, and would tell Susan that he didn't want to live with her anymore. Susan was heartbroken and at a loss as to what to do.

Example: John and Kim recently broke up. They were never married but have two children, Liam and Barry. One day, John is on the phone venting to his friend about Kim. Liam overhears John say all kinds of bad things about his mother. Liam is really angry at his mother for doing all these things and becomes hostile towards her. Both John and Kim are caught off guard by Liam's change in behavior, and chalk it up to the fact that kids sometimes act out when their parent's separate. Over time, Liam's anger grows, and his relationship with his mother becomes more and more tense and strained. Kim can't figure out what she did to deserve such treatment from her son. John's actions unintentionally led to a mild case of PAS, and can most likely be remedied if the parents are able to open up communication with Liam and find the source of his anger.

Parentification: This is a term that refers to a role reversal that is created when a parent attempts (intentionally or unintentionally) to turn their child into the parent and their caregiver. Parentification may happen for a wide number of reasons such as from untreated mental illness, substance abuse, depression, grief, personality disorders, etc.

When a child is turned into a parent, the child is then denied a childhood because they are having to take on adult responsibilities. The child oftentimes feels responsible for their parent's physical well-being by making sure they are eating, sleeping, getting up on time, or for their emotional well-being by listening to them complain about the other parent, or hearing about other adult concerns such as their parent's sex life, or their concerns about money, housing, and so on. Parentification can lead to a child developing an unhealthy way of relating to others—either needing to be taken care of or feeling the need to take care of others. Children who have been turned into young adults often come across as being "very mature for their age" when they are young, or later in life as the child matures, they may regress and be seen as "very immature for their age."

Example: Ron and Jane were married with an eight-year-old son, Cameron. Ron was in the Military, and whenever he had a deployment or was gone for more than a few days, Jane would tell Cameron that he was the man of the house while his father was gone, and that she needed him around as much as possible since his dad wasn't there. Jane would insist that Cameron sleep in bed with her so they could snuggle. She'd tell Cameron all about her adult problems with work and with Ron and how she feared he wouldn't come home from the war. Cameron would continually reassure his mother that everything was going to be okay and began to feel very protective of her, to where he felt guilty leaving her alone, even though he wanted to go play with his friends. He began putting his own wants and needs last and putting hers first.

Personality Disorder: A personality disorder is when a person has persistent problematic personality traits that are not due to substance abuse, medical issues, or could be seen as part of their developmental process (such as them being a demanding two year-old or a brooding teenager). These traits are so problematic and ongoing that they cause harm to their lives or to the lives of others (even if the person with the problematic behavior doesn't realize it's a problem).

Keep in mind that a person doesn't need to be diagnosed with (or have) a personality disorder in order for their behavior to be problematic or a deal breaker.

It's important that you are able to know yourself well enough to know what you need or want in your life and what you don't. If a person has any behavior that is destructive to you at any level, it's okay to distance yourself emotionally, physically, or both so that they don't have a negative impact on your life. Only you know what toxic behavior is for you and to what degree of distance you need from that person. There is no one size fits all answer.

Post Traumatic Growth (PTG): This is a concept that is associated with the positive psychology movement. Post-traumatic growth is the positive change resulting from the struggle with a major life crisis or a traumatic event. This struggle can bring a person to a higher level of awareness and overall functioning in their life that they may not have achieved in any other way.

Post-traumatic growth is not about healing from a traumatic event in the context of returning to the same life one had before the event happened. Life is always about growth and change, and we can only move forward and never backwards. A person can, however, go through a traumatic event and come out stronger and with a deeper appreciation for life because of it.

This mindset differs from traditional psychology in that more traditional approaches equate recovery with "resilience," which would be getting a person back to their baseline level of functioning before the traumatic event happened. The goal of post-traumatic growth is to replace resiliency with thriving, so that a person goes above and beyond resilience and is able to take what happened to them and use it for their highest and greatest good.

Here are some examples of post-traumatic growth:

-       A person who grows up with an abusive parent, and who has made the decision that they would never treat a child like they were treated, and who has moved forward to treat their own children with dignity, respect, and love.

-       A person who has been through an abusive relationship as an adult, and who has been able to take what happened and use it as a hard-learned lesson that they will never be treated with a lack of dignity or respect again. This new level of awareness helps them to improve their boundaries and relationships across the board and brings them to a new level of happiness and enjoyment.

172

- A person whose loved one was killed by a drunk driver and who now finds a deep sense of purpose and fulfillment speaking at high schools, educating teenagers about the consequences of drinking and driving.

Power and Control: These are two elements that are at the core of all forms of abusive behavior, and what is always sought after (either consciously or subconsciously) by an abusive person so that they can feel powerful by being in control of their target and of the situation.

Power and control is taken from others in covert and overt ways.

When most people think of power and control and abuse, they think of physical aggression and violence. However, two of the most abusive phrases are: "I love you" and "It's your fault." The reason these two phrases are so abusive, is that they often keep a person sucked into the relationship either out of hope that the abuser really does care about them and can change, guilt over wanting to leave such a damaged person, obligation to the abuser or to the relationship, or thinking is that the abuse is somehow their fault.

Abusive people tend to do what they want to do, whenever they want to do it, and they feel entitled and justified in doing so, even if their behavior causes hurt or harm to others (which it generally does). They lie and manipulate in order to get their way, and to keep power and control over their target or over how they are seen by others.

Everything that a narcissist says or does is designed to make them feel powerful and in control. In order to do that, they take away power and control from their target and from others. Power and control are gained through manipulative and abusive behavior that is done in verbal, emotional, psychological, sexual, financial, physical or spiritual ways, and often happens gradually over time. Once a person has been manipulated into thinking they are the problem, or that the narcissist's behavior isn't a problem, the target is at the mercy of the narcissist's erratic, destructive, and exploitative behavior and insatiable ego-gratifying power trips.

Example: John doesn't like that Jane is a Republican, because he is a Democrat. He continually picks fights with her and puts her down. If she tries to defend herself, John only gets louder and angrier; then he stops talking to her for several hours or several days. John gets power and control over Jane by shaming her, as well as by punishing her with the silent treatment.

Example: Doug volunteers at his local church as the youth minister. He uses the influence and trust of his position to gradually get power and control over people's perceptions of him so that in their mind he is a good, kind, godly man. He does this so that no one will suspect he is a child molester or believe his accusers if the truth is known.

Example: When Kara and James break up, he tells her that she will always belong to him, and that they aren't finished until he says so. His threatening behavior is his way of getting and keeping power and control over Kara by instilling fear in her so that she'll either stay or so she'll always be afraid of him.

Projection: Projection is a psychological defense mechanism when a person pushes their uncomfortable (and often repressed) thoughts, feelings, or actions onto someone else.

When narcissists project, they accuse their target of what they are thinking or doing (or planning to do), which is usually lying, cheating, manipulating, or abusing.

174

When a person projects their thoughts, feelings, and actions onto others, they are then able to convince themselves to some degree that the other person is really the one with the problematic behavior. And if they can convince themselves that their target has all this problematic behavior, then they feel justified in their abusive treatment of them.

A narcissist will generally project their problematic behavior onto others, because for them to fully be accountable for their cheating, lying, stealing, manipulating, and otherwise abusive or exploitative behavior they would have to adjust their view of themselves. But because they have such a high opinion of themselves, they are unable to accept that there could be anything wrong with them.

Example: Bob and Susan were married for seven years, and since the birth of their first child, Bob began to be more controlling. He insisted that Susan follow a budget (but he spent whatever he wanted), and he watched the mileage on her car. He also insisted that her mother and friends were all bad influences and that he didn't want her to spend so much time with them.

At first Susan chalked his behavior up to anxiety and stress from being a new dad. As time went on, he got worse, to the point where his yelling and screaming went on for hours, scaring her and upsetting the kids. But after every outburst, he would apologize and would return to being a great husband and father, surprising her with flowers or a weekend away, or giving the kids toys. He'd take pictures of these good behaviors and post them on Facebook. To the outside world, he looked like the world's greatest husband and father, but only those closest to him saw his abusive outbursts.

Bob's personality ran so hot and cold, it was like living with Dr. Jekyll and Mr. Hyde, and Susan often wondered if he was a great husband who had some bouts of bad behavior, or an abusive husband who had some bouts of good behavior.

Over the past few weeks, Bob began saying unsettling things to Susan, such as, "I had a bad dream that you died in a house fire," or "I'm concerned that the brakes on your car are going to go out." Susan didn't know what to make of this. Bob seemed legitimately concerned about her safety when he spoke of his fears. At times, Bob would also say he had a funny feeling she was going to disappear or be kidnapped. Susan couldn't shake the worry she felt when he said things like this. And even though he never physically harmed her, Susan felt that his talk about her death or disappearance was unsettling enough. She packed up the kids while he was out of town and left.

Example: Raul and Paola were dating for about a month when Paola's behavior turned from sweet and caring to suspicious and accusing. She accused Raul of cheating on her with his female co-workers. Raul didn't know what to make of this. He wasn't cheating on her with anyone, and he hadn't given her any reason to think that he would. He found himself continually trying to reassure her that he wasn't cheating and chalked up her bizarre and extreme behavior to her ex-boyfriend that she said cheated on her all the time.

What was especially odd was that Paola exhibited really suspicious behavior and had many male "friends" on social media that she messaged with at all hours of the night. And she took her phone with her everywhere she went and was especially protective of it when she was around Raul.

If Raul asked her about her behavior, she became incredibly defensive and angry and accused him of being jealous and controlling. Raul found her double standard to be crazy-making and exhausting. He wanted to trust her because she continually said how much she hated cheaters and how much she valued honesty in a relationship, but her actions didn't match up with that. Because her words and actions didn't line up, Raul found himself confused and continually wondering who had the problem. Was her behavior the problem? Was he right in thinking that she was acting suspicious? Or was her behavior normal, and he was jealous and controlling?

He later found out that she was cheating on him with one of her co-workers.

Example: Jim is covertly verbally, emotionally, and psychologically abusive to Michelle. Whenever she mentions that he's saying insensitive, rude, or cruel things, Jim denies it and blames her for being too sensitive, too emotional, and that she can't take a joke. The last time she brought up some issues, Jim said that he felt like she was being manipulative and abusive towards him! Michelle was shocked and became concerned about her behavior. She found herself wondering if perhaps she was manipulative and abusive and didn't know it.

Reactive abuse: This is when a target of abuse "reacts abusively" to an abusive person. A target often puts up with a lot of abusive behavior, because they either can't escape it, or because they've been conditioned through stonewalling, silent treatment, threats, or more abuse to put up with it. When a person reacts abusively to abuse, they often do so because they've reached their breaking point and lash out due to pent-up frustration and anger at being their emotional (or physical) punching bag. Once the target does react abusively, the abusive partner will portray themselves the victim of their target, exclaiming how abusive, crazy, or unhinged the target is. Reactive abuse is a delayed self-defense response. It is often extreme and is often disproportional to the current situation (it's the proverbial straw that broke the camel's back). A person can become reactive in ways that are either immediately aggressive, or they may begin to plot a way to hurt the abuser in order to settle the score. Reactive abuse is also one of a narcissist's favorite weapons against their target. They will push their target's buttons in ways that would push any sane person to their breaking point, and once their target does explode, they'll sit back and exclaim how unhinged, abusive, or crazy their target is.

Example: Jordan is a seventh-grader who has been bullied by Nick for the past year. Nick has made his life a living hell with his relentless teasing, taunting, name calling, and put downs. He continually told Jordan that he was a loser, and that he should kill himself. At first, Jordan tried talking to his parents about it, but they only told Jordan that he needs to stand up for himself; however, Jordan feels this would only make things worse. Jordan's teacher saw what was going on and much to Jordan's horror, she pulled both boys aside so they could all talk about it. Nick pretended not to know what he was doing was wrong, and gave an insincere apology to Jordan. Jordan could tell that Nick was enraged and that things were just going to get worse for him. Jordan felt trapped and over time he began to wonder if Nick was right about him being a loser and that maybe he should kill himself. No one seemed to take what was going on seriously, and his parent's wouldn't let him switch schools. One day, Nick took a picture of Jordan in his underwear in the locker room and texted them to other kids in the school, including the girl he liked. Jordan was infuriated and ran full-steam at Nick, pushing him to the ground, and beating him. He didn't stop until the gym teacher pulled him off of Nick.

Example: Sarah and Tim are dating. Tim makes flirty and inappropriate comments to other women, has a bunch of female "friends" that are all former lovers, is overly secretive with his phone as well as who he's going out with and where he's been. Another woman messages Sarah on Facebook telling her that her boyfriend is cheating on her. When Sarah confronts Tim about this, he stonewalls her, and refuses to admit anything. Sarah becomes more and more upset with Tim shutting down, and out of frustration and anger, she begins to yell at him demanding answers. Tim stays calm and overall "indifferent" as

Sarah becomes more and more upset. Sarah begins messaging all of his female "friends" on Facebook in an attempt to gain clarity as to whether or not Tim is having sex with them. The more Tim withholds clarity (and honesty), the more enraged Sarah becomes to the point where she begins throwing things, cussing at him, or shoving him. Tim tells Sarah that she is abusive and crazy. (And when their relationship eventually ends, odds are Sarah will be confused as to who really is the abusive one. She may even continue to return to the relationship as Tim continues to point out that she's not perfect, and look at everything he's had to put up with her.)

Example: Rhonda has a restraining order on her ex, Chris, which he has broken many times. However, he continues to text her and periodically shows up at her house. She is tired of him harassing her, tired of living in fear, and tired of the police and courts not being able to stop him. One day, Rhonda was at the grocery store when she saw Chris standing at the other end or the aisle, staring at her. He smiled and waved and walked off. Rhonda knew this wasn't a coincidence, as moved several hours away to get away from him. She chased him down in the store and began screaming and cussing at him.

Red Flags: Red flags are potential warning signs of a problematic person or situation.

Red flags are something we feel instead of something that we see because they are often more of a funny feeling that something is problematic, "off," or otherwise doesn't add up—even if we can't point to a specific reason as to why we feel that way. A red flag might happen based on a subtle micro-expression that flashes across a person's face, or they may say something that doesn't add up. A red flag might be more obvious, such as flashes of pushy, arrogant, or rude behavior, or boundary pushes.

Some red flags are more obvious than others, and what registers as a red flag for one person might not register as one for another. This is why it's important to listen to your gut instinct and to err on the side of caution. If something comes across your radar as problematic, then it doesn't matter if others don't see the situation in the same way, especially when it comes to abusive behavior because most people can't spot overt abuse, let alone covert abuse. A good gut check to make is to either think about the healthiest, most-grounded person you know, then to ask yourself what they would think or do in this situation, or to ask yourself what advice you'd give to your child or a friend if they were to be experiencing the same thing.

Example: Joan met Mick online. They recently began texting, and while he seemed like a fun and interesting guy, it struck her as odd that for their first date he invited her over to his house so he could cook her dinner. She felt like this was an inappropriate request, and that he was most likely looking for sex. Even if he wasn't looking for sex, she found his request odd, and it made her uncomfortable. She told him that she'd rather meet at a restaurant.

Example: Susan recently met David, her new upstairs neighbor in her apartment building. She wasn't quite sure what it was about him that gave her the creeps, but it was something. She decided to be a lot more aware of her surroundings when she was in and around her apartment.

Example: Mitchell was on his third date with Roger when a waitress accidentally spilled a drink on him. Roger instantly snapped and called her a "dumb bitch." Mitchell was shocked, and felt that not only was Roger's yelling and name calling a red flag, it was an instant deal breaker for him.

Reverse Projection: This is a slang term that refers to the distorted way targets of abuse tend to see their abuser. So where the psychological term "projection" refers to when a person projects all of their uncomfortable thoughts, feelings, or actions onto another who doesn't think, feel, or act that way, reverse projection is when targets project all of their good thoughts, feelings, and actions onto another who doesn't think, feel, or act this way.

Example: John and Lisa have been married for ten years. Even though John has a past history of aggression and abuse, Lisa continues to think that deep down John has the same morals and values that she has, and given enough love, therapy, religion, or rehab, he would treat her like she treats him. Lisa is projecting her good qualities onto John, even though his actions have shown that he does not share the same morals and values as Lisa.

Sadism: When a person gets pleasure from inflicting emotional and/or physical pain or humiliation on others, this is sadism. Many narcissists are sadistic and enjoy bringing their targets to the highest of emotional highs only to drop them to the lowest of emotional lows. In doing so, they feel smug, superior, and significant. Causing another person pain is, in many ways, the ultimate validation that a narcissist has power and control over their target and over the situation.

Example: Everything had been going wonderfully between Roger and Susan. He'd been talking a lot about taking a romantic trip over Valentine's Day weekend. Susan was getting more and more excited and really felt like Roger was her soul mate. She even wondered if he was going to propose. Then, out of nowhere, Roger broke up with her the night before Valentine's Day, saying that he needed his space. Susan was crushed. She didn't see this coming and couldn't believe that he could just end things so quickly and for no reason, especially when they seemed to have this intense soul mate connection. After four months of not hearing from him, he contacted her out of the blue like nothing had happened. They began dating again, but over the next six months, Susan began to notice that Roger had a pattern of waiting until either right before or right after some sort of major event (like a holiday, birthday, or vacation) to suddenly end things with her. At first, she wondered if he had issues with commitment, but the more frequently this happened, she began to wonder if it was more that he enjoyed seeing her in pain after he ruined these good times.

Self-love: To love something means to treat it with care. To love ourselves means to treat ourselves with care—which includes treating ourselves with dignity, respect, compassion, and value. For many people who have had either a narcissistic parent or partner in their life, the concept of self-love is one with which they really struggle. Generally because they've been led to believe that their wants, needs, and feelings need to come last—or don't matter at all, and that the narcissistic person's wants, needs, and feelings are the only priority.

A great way to tell how in (or out) of balance you are with self-love, is to check in with yourself on a regular basis to see if you are talking to or treating yourself the same way you would treat others.

Self-love is about loving yourself enough to make your wants, needs, and feelings a priority, and not putting yourself in harm's way. When a person loves themselves, they treat themselves with compassion and respect. Self-love goes hand-in-hand with self-care. It's knowing yourself well enough to know what your wants, needs, and feelings are—and knowing that those wants, needs, and feelings are valuable and worthy of being a priority in your life.

Self-love includes setting boundaries, limiting or cutting contact with toxic people or relationships, learning not to feel guilty for having an opinion or for asserting yourself, taking action from a place of interest and not out of obligation, fear, or guilt. It also includes spending time with people, places, and things that nourish and empower you and realizing that you are worthy of enjoying life, and being treated with care by yourself and others.

Silent Treatment: This is a verbally, emotionally, and psychologically abusive grooming technique when one person cuts off communication with another with the intention of sending the message of, "Don't confront me, challenge me, or try to set boundaries with me, or else I will freeze you out." The silent treatment can last hours, days, weeks, months, or even years, and is used to convey the narcissist's displeasure, disapproval and contempt toward the target, as well as to groom their target into behaving differently next time. Even though nothing is said, the message is loud and clear, "If you do this again, you will be punished until I determine you've had enough." During the time the target is being ignored, they often feel like they are in an emotional hell, left to twist in the wind wondering if they will ever hear from this person again. The loudness of the abusive person's silence can be so intense, that the target may find themselves walking on eggshells, trying to be a better partner, and offering up a stream of apologies for whatever it is they've done just so that person will talk to them again.

Narcissists aren't the only ones who give the silent treatment. Many people tend to resort to this when they aren't comfortable having an open and honest conversation about an issue. Regardless of whether the person is a narcissist or not, the silent treatment is still a problem, and not a healthy way to communicate. The silent treatment is not the same as "no contact." No contact is an appropriate response to abusive behavior, and is not designed to punish or groom a person; it's designed to be a self-protective measure taken to end the abusive treatment.

Example: Joanne found out about some flirty messages from her husband, Chris, to another woman. When she confronted him about it, he flew into a rage, then gave her the silent treatment, which lasted for three days. During this time, he wouldn't talk to her, touch her, or in any way acknowledge her presence. Joanne started crying, begging him to talk to her, and saying that she's sorry she got upset. She suggested that she should have asked him about it instead of being so confrontational. Chris glared at her and walked off. Three days later, Chris started talking to Joanne again and said that if she ever accused him of cheating again, he would leave. Relieved to have him talking to her again, Joanne profusely apologized and said that she would never doubt him again.

Example: Thomas sent Diane a text late one night telling her that he was at the bar with a friend and had some women buying him drinks. He said that he knew the reason they were doing this was because they could sense the confidence he had with a woman like her in his life. Diane thought his text was odd. Why were other women buying him drinks? And why was he okay with taking them if they were dating? She asked him about it, and told him that she wondered if he was trying to make her jealous. When she said this, he began yelling at her, blaming her for reading too much into it, and for being too insecure, jealous, and controlling. He went onto explain that everyone was buying each other drinks that night. Diane wondered, why he didn't say that to begin with, and why he framed the events in a way that felt like it was designed to make her jealous. It was as if he wanted to upset her, so he could then punish her for an emotion that she felt any normal person would have had. Thomas went on to say that he didn't know if he could handle her jealousy, then refused to talk to her or respond to her texts or phone calls for a week. When he began talking to her again, Diane said that she didn't like the silent treatment, to which Thomas replied that he wasn't giving her the silent treatment. He was giving her a chance to cool down because she was being too emotional.

Smear Campaign: A smear campaign is an unwarranted attack on the target's reputation, character and intent by making false accusations that are often believed by others. Narcissists are notorious for launching smear campaigns after the ending of a relationship, regardless of who ends it. It's their way of maintaining their public image, gathering the attention and sympathy from their enablers, and trying to destroy their target all at the same time. It's also how their level of denial and lack of self-awareness about their behavior shows itself, as a smear campaign lets others know (and reassures the narcissist) that they are not the problem.

Example: Kathy and Todd had been dating for about nine months. It has been an emotional roller coaster the whole time, but even though things could be bad, the good times were really good. He never felt this way about a woman before, and when Kathy dumped him out of the blue for another man that she swore was just a friend, he was devastated. When he asked her about this, she became angry and abusive, and dumped him without notice, without regard, or without giving him any type of answer or closure. He wondered what on earth happened and what he did that could have been so bad to make her leave. He couldn't wrap his mind around how things could go from being so great to nothing at all in the blink of an eye. He began texting and calling Kathy, begging her to talk to him, thinking that if he could just talk to her, they could work through whatever happened.

Unbeknownst to Todd, Kathy was showing other people all of his frantic texts as proof that he was obsessive and crazy. She twisted every text and email out of context and used them against him. Other people who had known Todd for years began to believe Kathy. Kathy also told people that she loved Todd, and she was very worried about him because he was just so unstable...not to mention she thought he might have an alcohol or drug problem. Todd did not. He soon found that many of his friends, family, and co-workers were stand-offish or outright ignoring him. He had no idea why or what was happening. It never occurred to him that Kathy would break up with him, let alone launch a smear campaign against him and try to destroy his life. He couldn't figure out what happened or how or why she was being so cruel.

Stockholm Syndrome: The term Stockholm Syndrome was coined by the criminologist and psychiatrist Nils Bejerot in 1973, after he assisted the police during a bank robbery in Stockholm in which four employees (three female and one male) were held hostage by two captors for six days. During their captivity, it was noted that the hostages had developed strong emotional attachments to their captors. Bejerot believed the attachments formed because the captors showed the captives crumbs of "kindness" during this time. For example, one captor told a hostage that he was going to shoot and kill him, but that he'd allow him to get drunk first. Another captor had a hostage sit with a noose around her neck for over twenty-four hours but allowed her food, water, and to go to the bathroom. These small acts of perceived kindness seemed to negate the fact that their lives were in danger. Another interesting twist was that the hostages also became upset with the police and the hostage negotiators, yelling at them that they were going to get them killed and to go away.

Even several decades after being released, it was discovered that some of the hostages were still defending their captors, and a few still kept in touch with them. One former hostage raised legal funds to aid in their captors' defense, and another periodically kept in touch with one of the captors after he got out of jail, and even had him over for several times for dinner with her family!

The hostages' seemingly bizarre behavior sparked off great interest and research into the phenomenon of emotional bonding between captors and captives in any dynamic. This type of emotional bonding is often referred to as "trauma bonding." These bonds are created and strengthened by the fear of extreme lows and the relief of the highs that happen in an unstable dynamic. This roller coaster of emotions, leaves the target feeling as though they are going through a lot with this other person, when the reality is that are being put through a lot by this other person.

Later psychologists wanted to know if what was witnessed in the Stockholm bank incident was a unique occurrence, or if it was more common than originally thought. Since then, studies have revealed that trauma bonds develop between all kinds of controlling and abusive partners and their targets, from a narcissistically abusive spouse to their partner, a child and their abusive parent, a rape victim and their rapist, a cult member and the cult leader, hostages/prisoners of war and their captives, sex workers and pimps, and so on. (Trauma bonds are covered more in depth in the "trauma bonds" section.)

Example: Samantha and Audrey had been "friends" since high school. During this time, their friendship was either really good or really bad, as Samantha had a pattern of being "difficult," controlling, and verbally and emotionally abusive. Oftentimes she demanded to know who Audrey was spending time with, or controlled what she wore or with whom she spoke. If Audrey spoke up for herself, Samantha would either call her names, give subtle put downs, or give her the silent treatment. Audrey felt compelled to stay in this friendship because Samantha wasn't this way all of the time. At times, Samantha could be very considerate, charming, and likable. Audrey was mistaking these moments of kindness as reassurance that Samantha really did value her as a friend, and felt that given enough reassurance, time, and understanding, Samantha would stop being so "difficult" and demanding and that their friendship could be saved. Audrey justified staying in the friendship because she thought Samantha needed her, and that deep down she was a good friend.

Example: Jody was in an abusive relationship with Phil. He often yelled at her, put her down, and told her she was worthless. Jody thought if she could just be nicer or approach Phil differently about concerns she had about the way he was treating her, he'd stop. She began to walk on eggshells trying harder and harder to avoid being abused, as well as to "earn" being treated with dignity and respect by him. Jody thought that if she could just become what he wanted her to be, their relationship could work. Jody didn't realize that what she was doing was problematic; she thought that all relationships were about making compromises. The more time went on, the more abusive Phil became. Whenever Jody tried to talk to friends or her therapist about what was going on, she became defensive when they encouraged her to leave. Her common response was, "I know he can be awful…but I love him."

Stonewalling: This term refers to a person shutting down emotionally and becoming as communicative as a stone wall. When a person stonewalls, they will not budge and there is a general refusal on their end to communicate or cooperate. Stonewalling may or may not be accompanied by the "silent treatment." Many targets report that when their partner stonewalls them it's like "trying to have a conversation with a brick wall" because their partner won't give any information, clarity, validation, closure, or understanding about their behavior. They may change the subject, or announce that this subject is closed and that their partner is living in the past (therefore shifting the blame to where it's now the partner's problem).

Being stonewalled can feel emotionally exhausting for the target because they are left alone to do all the healing from their partner's selfish, insensitive, and hurtful behavior. And that's the point. The emotional manipulator doesn't want to deal with their partner's emotions or with the inconvenience of having to explain themselves or justify their actions, so they don't give out any further information. They simply shut down communication. The result is that the partner gets worn out playing detective and feeling like they need to draw out the truth. They generally give up and realize that they will never get the answers they want. If they are going to stay in the relationship, then they will have to settle for not getting the full truth, let alone closure from their partner.

Example: Cherie confronts John about his cheating. John won't give her any answers or any information about who the woman is, when and why this happened, or any other details that she hasn't already discovered. When Cherie wants answers, he refuses, and spins the conversation back onto her, pointing out that she isn't perfect either. This is maddening for Cherie, because John will not stay on the issue at hand and keeps spinning the conversation in many different ways.

Sweet/Mean Cycle: This is a cycle where a narcissist's behavior swings from being nice or normal to abusive, silent, or cruel. The person on the receiving end of this tends to feel that everything was fine; then their partner's behavior does a sharp and unexpected turn and they become abusive or withdrawn. Like any kind of problematic behavior, this sweet/mean cycle, can be done to both children and adults. These highs and lows (also known as intermittent reinforcement) put a person on an emotional roller coaster, and can lead to a lot of confusion about the type of person they are dealing with, to the point where they can't tell if this person is their soul mate or their biggest nightmare. The lows of the mean part of this cycle often happen around highly emotional or important events for the target, such as a birth, death, illness, birthday, holiday, recital, graduation, and so on. Or they can happen out of the blue. Many people who have been in a dynamic with an emotional manipulator have experienced this sweet and mean cycle so often that they brace themselves around important events because history proves that the manipulator consistently causes a scene or otherwise ruins celebrations or get-togethers.

To the outside world (even to those in the inside world), the sweet side of the sweet/mean cycle looks like the person is sincerely sorry because they often make over-the-top (sometimes very public) displays of apologizing. Their behavior has the added crazy-making of creating "flying monkeys" out of other people who mistake these acts of sweetness as sincerity. They don't realize this is all part of the cycle of narcissistic abuse.

Example: Beth promises her son, Jarred, that she will be there to see him perform in the school play. She tells him a few hours before that she can't make it because her new boyfriend made plans to take her to dinner. Her son is crushed. The child's father tries to comfort him, but Jarred is understandably upset. Later at the play, Beth shows up with a big sign that says, "I love you Jarred!" She waves it in the crowd. Jarred experiences an emotional high and feels that his mother really does care. Over time, Beth continues to exhibit behavior that swings between incredibly selfish and incredibly considerate. The child can't figure out where he stands with his mother, or who she even is. He can't decide if she's mean or if she's nice.

Example: Jane catches her husband, Charles, cheating again. This time, Charles promises that things will change. He will no longer cheat or lie, and he will be the man that she needs him to be. He sends his wife three-dozen roses while she's at work. Two weeks later, he leaves her on the morning of her birthday, saying that he's been unhappy for a while. He can't take how Jane continues to bring up the past, and wants a divorce. Jane is devastated and spends the next four months in therapy trying to cope with her intense feelings of guilt, remorse, depression, and confusion. As soon as she is starting to feel more evened out emotionally, Charles shows up two days before Christmas with presents for her and toys for the kids, saying that he wants another chance, and that Jane should know that he would never really divorce her because he loves her and the kids. The kids are all excited that their father is back and has brought them toys. They forgive him for being gone for four months and not calling. Charles tells them that "Mommy and Daddy will never get divorced because family is about forgiveness and commitment." Jane is angry, happy, sad, and confused by what she's experiencing, but tries to push aside all her negative feelings in order to focus on having a nice Christmas for the kids.

Target: A target is a person who is the focus of abusive behavior.

Example: Billy is in ninth grade and is being bullied by Scott and his friends. Billy is the target of their abuse.

Example: Susan's mother has always been verbally and physically abusive but primarily to her. Susan grew up feeling that her two other siblings could do no wrong, while Susan could do nothing right. Susan was the target of her mother's abuse.

Example: Ken and Serena are dating. Ken is verbally, emotionally, and psychologically abusive toward Serena, but he is kind, charming, and friendly toward her friends and coworkers.

Trauma Bonding: Trauma bonding is a term that refers to the strong emotional attachment or bond between an abused person and their abuser which is formed due to the bad times followed by the relief of the good times that a person often experiences during the cycle of abuse. A target will often try to walk on eggshells in an attempt to avoid the abuse and to keep the relationship going as smoothly as possible. The walking on eggshells, as well as the highs and lows are known as "intermittent reinforcement."

Because abusive people are generally not "actively" abusive one-hundred percent of the time, the target clings to the moments of the narcissist's good behavior as proof that everything is going to be okay and that the relationship can work.

One way the target attempts to cope with all the problematic behavior (and ease all the cognitive dissonance that they are experiencing) is to shift their thinking from "me" to "we." This way, the abuse isn't something that happens to them alone. Instead, it is a shared experience with their partner. It is an ordeal that they survive together. The target feels that they are "going through so much together," instead of seeing it as being put through so much by this person. This new mindset is often fed by manipulations and lies by the narcissist, who may claim that "going through so much" is what relationships are all about, or that real relationships stay together no matter what. When this mindset shift is made, a bond forms between the narcissist and their target, as there are now three elements in the relationship: the abuser, the target, and the abusive or exploitative behavior. The problem is that there really is no third element; the abusive person and their behavior are one in the same.

The target often continues to seek reassurance and comfort from the abuser, thinking, "He/she caused pain, and only he/she can take it away." This is because when people experience trauma/abuse, they instinctively seek reassurance that everything is going to be okay. When they have become conditioned (or have been isolated) to only turn to their partner, then they are sent on a confusing and chemically induced emotional rollercoaster to where the good times releases oxytocin and dopamine, which are two chemicals the brain releases that facilitate both attachment and bonding. And the bad times are full of stress and fear of their partner hurting them (either physically or emotionally by leaving). During these bad times, cortisol and the chemicals that compose adrenaline (norepinephrine and epinephrine) are released. The result is the lows switch on a person's fight or flight mechanism, which is then deactivated or calmed down by the highs of the oxytocin and dopamine.

These ups and downs often create feelings of craving and dependency, much like an addict feels when they are going through withdrawal. These feelings can be really intense (unlike anything they've ever experienced) and can often be confused for love. A person may feel addicted to this abusive person and wonder what the hell is wrong with them and why they still miss or love this person, or why they can't stop thinking about them. Many people also report feeling "numb" or "flat" after a relationship with a narcissist, especially if they are not aware that they went through abuse, or they feel it was somehow their fault and that they lost their soulmate. They worry that they'll never feel this way about anyone again. Or they may leave this relationship, but then unbeknownst to them, be primed for abuse as they are easily hooked by the intense highs (and resulting oxytocin and dopamine) that are manufactured during the love bombing that so often accompanies an abusive relationship.

Example: John yells and belittles Sarah for feeding her dog a piece of her meal. He raises his voice and tells her that he's disgusted by letting her dog eat her leftovers and that she has no class, and he doesn't know what he's doing with someone like her. John's reaction and attitude catch Sarah off guard, and she feels confused, upset, and scared by his behavior. They finish dinner in silence, and when she gets up to clear the table John tells her how sexy she is in her new jeans, and how he's so lucky to have her as a girlfriend. Sarah quickly goes from a low to a high and experiences a tremendous amount of relief when she does.

Example: Starting as far back as she can remember, Nancy has always been the target of her mother's abuse. Nancy spent a large portion of her childhood walking on eggshells around her mother and continually trying to simultaneously avoid being abused and earning her love. She often wondered what it was about her that was so unlovable to make her mother act this way. Any crumb of kindness that her mother gave to her was treasured by Nancy, and used as proof to her that her mother really did care. It was these crumbs that kept Nancy continually trying to make her relationship with her mother work…and kept her in the cycle of abuse.

Triangulation: Triangulation happens when some form of drama or chaos is created between three people. This can happen in any number of ways, but perhaps the most common are when a narcissist turns two other people against each other while putting themselves in the middle, or where the narcissist aligns themselves with one of the people, creating an "us against you" situation.

A narcissist generally triangulates others for three main reasons: to escape being accountable for their behavior; because it makes them feel important by watching others fight over them or get caught up in the drama they have created, or simply because it's fun for them to watch this chaos unfold.

Example: John is married to Sally, and he is having an affair with Elaine, whom he met through an online dating site. Elaine thinks that John is separated, and during the few weeks that they've been dating, John has been the best boyfriend she's ever had. John tells her that they are still living together, but only because Sally is really manipulative and that he's needing to be very careful about how he goes about leaving so she doesn't drain his accounts. He professes to be a man of his word and that he has tried to really make his marriage work. He also adds that he and his wife haven't been intimate in months, and that they are in separate bedrooms, but now that he's met Elaine, he has the motivation to move out. These remarks elicit pity from Elaine for his bad marriage, and turn her against Sally. His words also imply that if Sally wasn't in the picture they could have a future together.

Then Sally (who thinks John's cheating is over, and that their marriage is improving) catches John cheating...again. After weeks of him denying it and accusing Sally of being jealous, paranoid, and having trust issues, he finally caves in and admits to having sex with Elaine when Sally sees text messages between them. He tells Sally that he met Elaine while he was out at lunch one day and that she threw herself at him—but that she means nothing to him and it was only a one-night stand. He tells her that Elaine is crazy and obsessed with him and that he doesn't know how to get rid of her. These remarks make Elaine the problem, and elicit pity and hope from Sally. Sally is now thinking that if Elaine wasn't in the picture, they could go back to having a good marriage.

Now the two women are fighting each other, each thinking that the other one is the problem, and each one thinking that they will have a great relationship with John as soon as the other woman is out of the picture. John is free of all accountability, because each woman is blaming the other one, and he is now the center of attention, and the "prize" to be fought over. He uses both women as a source of "narcissistic supply" because now he feels significant because these two women are fighting over him, all the while he gets to sleep with both of them and is making each of them think that the other woman is the problem and not him.

Example: Ted and Susan are recently divorced and have a ten-year-old son, Brian. Ted tells Brian that he can no longer afford to pay for his soccer lessons because he has to pay Susan child support. The result of this is that Ted creates hurt and hard feelings between Susan and Brian.

Example: Georgia and her boyfriend Ben go out every weekend to a bar or to a party. And almost every weekend Ben gets into a fight with another guy over Georgia. What he doesn't realize is that when he's not looking, Georgia is flirting with other men, and then when they buy her a drink or try to dance with her, Ben gets upset and a fight ensues. The whole time, Georgia sits back and soaks up the attention as it makes her feel attractive and important to have men fighting over her.

Trigger: A trigger is a sight, smell, sound, word, touch, taste, place, or person that sets off an emotional flashback to an event. Flashbacks can relate to a positive or negative event. The trigger is often not seen by others, and can be as seemingly harmless as the smell of baking bread, or daisies blowing in the wind, or more obvious, such as the home in which the abuse took place, seeing the same type of alcohol on the shelf that their abuser drank, seeing the same type of car that they drove, meeting someone who has the same name, or hearing a certain sound such as a loud noise, or "their" song.

Example: John was verbally and emotionally abused by his mother when he was a child. After she was done berating and belittling him, she would tell him that she "loved him anyhow, even though he was so rotten." John is now dating Brenda, and last night he accidentally knocked over a vase with flowers in it. He apologized for his clumsiness, and began cleaning it up. Brenda was surprised by how upset he was, and in an attempt to reassure him, she told him not to worry, that she loved him anyway (not knowing his mother used to tell him the same thing after she abused him). John felt his chest tighten, and his fists began to clench. Tears sprang to his eyes. His reaction caught both him and Brenda off guard.

Example: Michelle was in an abusive relationship with Todd who drove a black pickup truck. Even though it has been several years since she last saw or heard from Todd, whenever she sees a black pickup truck, she feels intense panic and anxiety.

Well-Intended Bad Advice: In terms of an abusive relationship, well-intended bad advice is advice that people give with good intentions, but this advice leads to a series of disastrous outcomes. I find it helpful to think of well-intended bad advice as "thought holes." A thought hole impacts a person's thinking much like a pot hole impacts a person's vehicle. Meaning, if you hit one, it can either cause a lot of damage or it can make you lose control and wind up in a ditch. And much like a pot hole, you might not see a thought hole coming. But once you know about them, you can spot them and avoid them.

Here are some examples of some very common (and very minimizing and invalidating) well-intended bad advice (or thought holes):

"It could always be worse."

While things could always be worse, that doesn't make an abusive situation somehow acceptable or not a problem.

"It's important to keep them in your life because, after all, they are your parent/spouse/child/boss/best friend since childhood, etc."

Abusive behavior is abusive behavior. When a person cuts off contact with a parent, sibling, child, friend, or anyone else due to their abusive behavior, it's because they are tired of being abused and trying to protect themselves psychologically, emotionally, or physically. A person needs to do what they need to do in order to stay safe and sane. It's okay and healthy for people to protect themselves.

"No one is perfect."

While no one may be perfect, not all people are abusive, and being treated abusively isn't okay.

"It's important to forgive and forget."

Forgiveness has nothing to do with forgetting what happened or allowing a dangerous or destructive person back into your life. Forgiveness means to release the anger you have toward someone who has wronged you, and to truly release anger toward someone who has caused tremendous damage in your life is a process, it's not an event.

However, it's important to realize that while the anger can feel all-consuming and overwhelming, it is also a normal and healthy response to an abnormal and unhealthy situation, and it is an important stage in healing.

Anger is an important stage in healing because it is often the first step towards getting back into alignment with how you feel—especially if your feelings about how you've been treated were continually invalidated or minimized. And because this anger can feel so hard won, many people struggle with wanting to let it go. They may also struggle with fear that releasing this anger will potentially cause them to forget (or minimize) what happened and lead them to be revictimized by this person.

It's important to never forget how an abusive person behaved. This isn't holding a grudge or living in the past; it's acknowledging a person's true colors so you can take appropriate action to keep yourself safe so they don't treat you like this again.

"Who are you to judge?"

When you decide a person's behavior is toxic to you (or even simply not what you want in your life), this isn't about judging them, it's about discerning who you keep in your life, especially in your inner circle. It's critically important that a person know themselves well enough so that they can discern the difference between what nourishes them from what is toxic to them and act accordingly.

Withholding: This term refers to one of the many ways a narcissist punishes their target for disagreeing with them, challenging them, or setting boundaries. A narcissist will commonly withhold affection, attention, important information, access to money/child support, or the target's ability to get a good night's sleep. Withholding can be done in ways that are overt, such as withholding attention or affection (commonly sex) or, "You don't need to know the bank account information" (when they have a joint account or are married). Withholding can also be done in more covert ways such as making a lot of noise, turning the lights on, or trying to engage the target in a fight or long conversations when they have an important job interview or an early flight the next day. In this way, the narcissist is "withholding" sleep from them.

Withholding is also commonly (and very subtly) used early on in the relationship in order to groom targets into submission. Things may be going great in the relationship, but then start to take a turn when all of a sudden the target starts feeling that the narcissist is pulling their affection away either for no reason, or because they had some sort of disagreement (which could have been as simple as disagreeing on what to have for dinner). They may find themselves in a scramble to get their attention and affection back. The result is that the target learns early on to always agree with them or there will be hell to pay and eggshells to walk on.

This is especially the case with a narcissistic parent who may withhold love, food, attention, affection, emotional support, basic health or school needs, etc. as punishment for challenging them or for the child simply being upset with them. This behavior may start as early as soon after the child is born, as the narcissist feels resentful that the infant is demanding to be fed or changed, or that the infant is getting more attention and compliments than they are.

Narcissists also commonly withhold basic needs from their children as a way to punish their target for leaving them. They may refuse to have contact with that child if that child is living with the other parent, or they may refuse to pay child support or for the child's extracurricular activities, attend school functions, take the child to the doctor, change their diaper, or make sure they are fed. They may drop off the child, telling the other parent that these things are their problem and responsibility, or that they can't afford it (when they can). Targets who have divorced a narcissist quickly learn that any issue that the narcissist has with them will be taken out on their child too.

Chapter 6: The Cycle of

Narcissistic Abuse

Narcissistic abuse tends to run in a fairly predictable pattern, or cycle of idealize, devalue, discard. While the phases are always the same, every target will experience this cycle differently, meaning that they will experience each phase differently and for different lengths of time. This is not only because each abuser is different, but also what works for each target is also different. In addition, because narcissists tend to have a steady stream of "supply" in their pipeline, each "supply" is in a different phase in the cycle at all times, and oftentimes these phases overlap.

So for example, if you were recently discarded, you might have noticed that the new supply is being "idealized" (or treated) in all the ways that the narcissist would never treat you. Perhaps the narcissist would never post pictures of the two of you on Facebook, but three days into their new relationship, their Facebook page is filled with pictures of them and their new supply. Or perhaps they refused to go on a vacation with you, but now they are vacationing with the new supply. Or perhaps you were with them for five years, and they never bought you an engagement ring, but now their new supply has the ring you picked out—and only after dating them for three weeks! Odds are this feels like salt is being poured in your wound…and it's meant to. So while the narcissist is idealizing their new supply/target, they are also getting the sadistic satisfaction of continuing their devalue stage with you.

Three Phases of Narcissistic Abuse

Idealize

The idealize phase is how targets often get sucked into (or back into) the cycle of narcissistic abuse. This phase often includes love bombing, mirroring (where the narcissist "mirrors" their target's thoughts, feelings, and actions back to them, which creates a feeling of meeting a perfect partner), rushing intimacy (having sex within the first few dates, sharing deeply personal things about their life—actions that overall create a sense of deep trust that hasn't been earned).

During this idealization phase, things often move quickly, and a whirlwind romance or connection (or reconnection) of some sort is formed. And while the target realizes that things are moving a little too fast, or seem a little too good to be true, they also tend to feel a deep and sincere connection to the narcissist. Oftentimes the idealize phase involves over-the-top romantic gestures, but not always.

The common theme with the idealize phase is that the target has become the narcissist's main focus, and getting their undivided attention can make a person feel very loved and important—especially if they are lonely, grew up never feeling loved or important, or are recently out of an abusive relationship. If romance is involved, then the target may feel as though they've won the relationship lottery and have met their soul mate. They may feel swept off their feet with all of the flattery, attention, and intense love that they once thought only existed in the movies. They also may feel that the narcissist is moving too quick, being immature with their professions of love, wanting to spend too much time with them, and falling for them much too soon.

In addition, the narcissist is also most likely talking about how their former partner was abusive, manipulative, crazy, bipolar, jealous, or obsessed with them, or how they grew up with an abusive parent. They may have text messages to show just how obsessive and "crazy" their former partner was, and have created a story about how they are the victim of their former partner's behavior. They may claim that their former partner faked abuse, cheated on them, won't let them see their child, or filed false charges against them. The result of this is that the new target is now turned against the former target, and of course, the new target is going to believe the narcissist; after all, they seem like a great person. It can be difficult to tell if someone is telling the truth about their previous relationships. Even if the narcissist was abused before, it doesn't make their abusive behavior somehow okay or workable. The only way to know for sure is to give the relationship time and to keep your eyes open for red flags.

Because this idealize stage can feel like something that only happens once in a lifetime, a target may find themselves nervous that they might not live up to the narcissist's high view of them, and they don't want to let them down or ruin a good thing. The narcissist will also most likely build the target up and talk about how beautiful, intelligent, capable, or amazing they are. The target may feel like they are being put on a pedestal and unworthy of all this praise and flattery. The narcissist may continue to flatter them and tell them it's a shame that the other people in their life never felt this way about them. The target may feel that maybe all of their hesitations about being treated like this are due to their low self-esteem, and that the way the narcissist is treating them is what a healthy relationship must feel like. …And the narcissist may feed into this, telling them that the target's hesitations are due to their past with abusive people or their low self-esteem, and that they have their guard up because they are scared to be loved.

Over time this idealization phase slowly morphs into the devalue phase, and the narcissist's attention and affection starts to dwindle, and is slowly replaced with lying, cheating, stealing, or other forms of abusing. The target is confused when this starts to happen, and often finds themselves in a scramble to earn back the narcissist's attention and affection. When the devalue stage and the abuse does happen, it's often done so gradually and so stealthily that the target often feels how they are being treated is their fault.

Devalue

The devaluing or grinding down of the target often starts as subtle put-downs, mean or insensitive criticism, brutal hones-ty, sarcasm, cruel "joking," or outbursts of anger (or rage) that are disproportionate to the situation. When the target brings up concerns about this behavior, they are accused of being too sensitive, too emotional, controlling, manipulative, unable to take a joke, or somehow unable to handle the truth. This behav-ior is usually peppered with the abusive person planting seeds of insecurity regarding the relationship, jealousy, or inadequa-cy, along with squirrelly or confusing behavior such as talking to their exes, messaging with new people online, hiding their phone, or making comments about how attractive other people are.

Over time, the narcissist's abusive behavior grows into name calling, yelling, screaming, belittling, siphoning household funds (taking on debt the other person doesn't know about or approve of), cheating, lying (telling lies both little and big, even when the truth would work better), giving the silent treatment, stonewalling, becoming physically "rough," using guilt, shame, or obligation to get sex out of their partner, or to get their part-ner to do things they aren't comfortable with sexually.

This behavior becomes more frequent, and the target may begin to notice a pattern. Mainly, that anytime they disagree with or challenge the narcissist in any way, there is hell to pay. The narcissist may also use guilt, shame, fear, or obligation in-volving God, religion, family, or commitment about what their partner's role is in order to keep power and control over them.

Like I mentioned before, not everyone experiences the phases of narcissistic abuse in the same way. Some people don't experi-ence such an overt devalue phase, or even such an overt ideal-ization phase. What they may experience instead is a charming partner, everything going seemingly fine in their relationship, and then their partner's double life comes out. And like with overt abuse, targets in these relationships will also begin to no-tice a pattern. The narcissist in their life might periodically insist on a divorce out of the clear blue, or provoke a fight around holidays or birthdays which results in the narcissist breaking up with them or giving them the silent treatment. Targets may come to realize that whenever this is happening, it's generally because the narcissist is off cheating…again, or because they like to stay the center of attention or because they like to ruin other people's good times because it makes them feel important. But make no mistake, while the target isn't directly experiencing a devalue stage, it's still being done…behind their back. The narcissist's new supply is generally being told about how manipulative, difficult, controlling, bipolar, or crazy the narcissist's other partner is.

The idealize phase lures a person into the relationship, and the devalue phase is how the narcissistic person works towards getting and keeping power and control over their target by abusing, using, exploiting, or neglecting them. And again, the whole time this is going on, the target, thinking it's their fault, starts trying harder and walking on more eggshells in an attempt to win back the narcissist's love in order to get the abusing, using, lying, cheating, exploiting, or neglecting to stop.

Discard

The discard phase often happens out of the blue. The narcissist may suddenly (and cruelly) break up with their target with little to no notice or regard, often blaming the target for the relationship ending. When the discard happens, the target is often left feeling emotionally devastated, numb, bitter, confused, and angry as hell, as they've put up with so much bad behavior from the narcissist, they feel they should have earned the narcissist's love and commitment.

If a narcissist is sadistic, then the discard phase may happen (repeatedly) around important times when the target needs them the most, such as the target or their children were recently diagnosed with a major illness, they just bought a house or car together—one that the target can't afford on their own, or they recently got pregnant or adopted a child. Or the discard might happen around what should be joyous times, such as the holidays, or birthdays. The reason for the discard at these times is that it creates an especially intense emotional reaction in the target, making the narcissist feel really important by being able to hurt them this much. In addition, if the discard is done after the target has somehow deeply intertwined their life with the narcissist (getting pregnant, buying a house, getting a pet) the narcissist knows that the target is going to be much more likely to continue to take them back, as they now have them on the hook.

When the narcissist does move on, they either blame the target, or they blame themselves (but they aren't sincere—they do so in order to make the target beg them to stay so they can work on things). When the target is blamed, they often see a staggering degree of the narcissist's "indifference" (lack of empathy and remorse) which can come across as confusing, incredibly hurtful, or terrifying.

It is also very common for narcissists to have multiple people in their supply pipeline, so they tend to move on very fast—often dating someone new within the week, erasing all trace of their old relationship and replacing it with pictures of how happy they are with their new partner. This leaves the former target beyond devastated, and wondering how the narcissist could move on so quickly, and if their relationship ever meant anything to them.

What Many People Experience After a Relationship with a Narcissist Ends

- You may find a staggering amount of manipulation and

lies from the narcissist.

- The narcissist may move on quickly, as if your relationship meant nothing.

- The narcissist may blame you for everything and claim to be the victim of you.

- The narcissist may become upset that you don't want to work things out, and may try to use guilt, obligation, sympathy, or religion to get you to stay—making it seem as though you are the one who isn't committed to the relationship. Even though all of their behavior (or at least the behavior that you found out about) was full of lying, cheating, stealing, manipulating, and/or abusing and otherwise relationship-ending behavior.

- You may wonder if you really were the problem, or if you are somehow abusive, manipulative, or a narcissist—especially if they continually told you this.

- You may be fearful that they will change for the next person.

- You may feel enraged, frustrated to tears, or re-victimized because no one seems to understand, or worse, treats what you went through as nothing more than a bad breakup.

- You may feel angry and resentful that they moved on easily, especially if you feel your life is blown to pieces.

- You may feel angry and resentful that no one else sees their abusive behavior, or that others make excuses for their abusive behavior.

- You may feel that you don't know what normal is, or that

you don't trust your judgment about people.

- You may feel paranoid, anxious, depressed, and hyper-vigilant, or that you don't know who else might hurt you (emotionally or physically).

- You might get well-intended bad advice from people who encourage you to give the manipulator another chance, or to continue trying to make things work.

- You may feel outraged, resentful, and re-victimized by people who give you well-intended bad advice or who don't seem to understand or take your situation seriously, especially if this comes from a therapist/mental health clinician, domestic violence agency, police, or courts/attorneys.

- You may feel ashamed, embarrassed, and angry that you didn't see the abuse for what it was at the time, and for staying as long as you did.

- You may feel stupid and embarrassed for not seeing the red flags of the major signs that they were abusive.

- You may find that they are talking to your friends and family and making themselves out to be the victim of you.

- You may wonder if you will ever heal from this, or if you will be forever broken.

- You may be terrified to date or to open up to someone again or scared that you will become the target of another narcissist.

- You may want to isolate and avoid spending time with friends and family.

- You may have a really hard trusting people, and every-thing may feel like a red flag (you feel "hyper-vigilant").

- You may feel that no one understands, and when you do open up you feel revictimized by people telling you that you should have left earlier or that you should be glad they are out of your life.

Please know that you are not crazy; you've been traumatized and manipulated. I highly recommend getting into a support group with people who have been through this, as getting clarity and hearing the experiences of others will give you a lot of validation that you aren't the only one going through this, and that you didn't cause it or deserve it.

Chapter 7: Frequently Asked Questions

What is the difference between a narcissist and a selfish jerk?

The difference has to do with whether this behavior is an event or a pattern. A narcissist is someone who has a long-lasting pattern of selfish jerk type behavior, which tends to include any or all of the following: being rude, insensitive, and hurtful, chronic lying, chronic cheating, manipulating, triangulating, stealing/siphoning household funds, using, exploiting, and having overall crazy-making behavior and a jaw-dropping lack of sincere insight into the fact that any of this behavior is a problem for others, as well as a lack of sincere empathy and remorse for their actions. Narcissists don't take accountability for their actions, and if they do, it's not sincere. They also tend to get very upset when challenged or confronted, or when boundaries are set with them.

A selfish jerk is someone who might be behaving narcissistically, but their behavior is usually an event, meaning it happens once. If their problematic behavior is brought to their attention they are fully accountable for it, and work to fix the damage done by their behavior, and the behavior doesn't continue to happen. If their behavior is a pattern, then they may or may not be a narcissist, but they do have problematic behavior.

Remember, a person doesn't need to have a full-out personality disorder in order for things to be a problem. If a person is continually crazy-making, toxic, draining/exhausting, or otherwise agitating or bad for your mental health (or safety), these are reasons enough to distance yourself from them.

How do I know for sure they have Narcissistic Personality Disorder?

In terms of getting a formal diagnosis for Narcissistic Personality Disorder, the only way is for a mental health clinician to do an evaluation. However, getting a narcissist in for a diagnosis, then making sure the clinician won't be manipulated by them can be an exercise in frustration and crazy-making in and of itself. Many narcissists do an award-winning job of manipulating people and becoming a social chameleon to say and do the right things, even going so far as to come across as sincere, accountable, and insightful, especially in front of a mental-health clinician. There is a saying out there that goes, "Narcissistic Personality Disorder is the only disorder in which the patient is left alone, and those closest to them are treated."

And while it can be validating to get a diagnosis that yes, in fact, this person has a personality disorder, the reality is that diagnosing personality disorders is not an exact science. You can ask ten different mental health professionals and potentially get ten very different diagnoses. Not to mention that the terms in the DSM change often. So for example, there has been talk of removing the term "Narcissistic Personality Disorder" from the DSM. This does not mean that the behaviors are not problematic, or that narcissism doesn't exist. It simply means that the term may change to be combined with something else, or may simply be renamed altogether. These changes can be very confusing and problematic for people who are relying on a diagnosis for validation of what they are experiencing.

If a person has a personality disorder, it means that they have a handful of persistently problematic personality traits that cause problems in their lives (whether or not they see it) and in the lives of others.

For these reasons, I would encourage you to shift your focus from needing a formal diagnosis to tell you that something is problematic and more to focusing on what problematic behavior is, and getting in tune with what's a deal breaker for you.

I think many people who ask this question struggle with black or white thinking that if a person has a diagnosable personality disorder then (and only then) is it a problem, but if they don't have a diagnosis, then their behavior is somehow fixable. The reality is that all behavior is on a spectrum, and if a person has persistently problematic behavior, and they aren't sincerely motivated to change it then it's a problem worthy of being a deal breaker.

Could I be a narcissist and not know it?

After reading about narcissism, it's really common for people to see some of these behaviors within themselves and to be concerned that they might be a narcissist. It's also very common for a person to get out of an abusive relationship, and for the narcissist to continually tell them that they are abusive, manipulative, and the narcissist...and to wonder if this is true.

However, if you are reflecting on your own behavior, and are concerned about certain elements of it, then odds are you are not a narcissist (as narcissists don't think they have a problem). You might have some behaviors that are problematic, but if you are aware of them and are sincerely motivated to work on them, then go for it. Don't let anyone define you or tell you what you can or can't change as far as your personality or behavior goes. They don't know what's possible for you; only you do.

What's the difference between a narcissist's problematic behavior and "normal" problematic behavior?

Problematic behavior is problematic behavior, and it's all equally damaging. However, narcissistic people tend to have a lot more of it on a much more consistent basis, and when confronted about how their behavior is harmful to others, they don't sincerely care. They believe that they are justified in treating others how they see fit. If people have a problem with being treated badly, then they either deny or minimize their mistreatment of the other person, or they own up to it, claiming the other person is to blame, or that they deserved it.

A person with "normal" problematic behavior might accidentally hurt someone's feelings. If this is brought to their attention, they apologize, and make sure to not let it happen again. They take the feelings of those around them into consideration and have open, honest, sincere, solutions- oriented communication and work to resolve differences and hurt feelings. They don't deny, blame, punish, or overall devalue others if they have a problem with their behavior.

If you tell a person that they are behaving in a way that is hurtful, and they blame you for being too sensitive, or somehow deserving to be treated in a hurtful way—especially if they continue doing it—then that is a big problem, worthy of being a deal breaker.

How can I tell if I'm in an abusive relationship?

An abusive relationship is one that involves any kind of abusive behavior, whether it is verbal, emotional, psychological, sexual, financial, spiritual, or physical (see the definition of "abuse" in Chapter 4, for details of each).

In most abusive relationships there is more than one form of abuse happening. However, because the person in an abusive relationship may be used to experiencing abusive behavior, it becomes their new normal. They may justify this acceptance by saying things like, "That's just how we fight." At this point, the abuse may not register as problematic at all, and it often takes someone else telling them that they are in an abusive relationship, telling them that they are in danger, or them experiencing such over-the-top, undeniably abusive behavior for it to register on their radar as abuse.

Can a narcissist change?

The vast majority of clinicians out there will tell you that a narcissist cannot and will not change. I see a lot of people get pondering this question, and they spend a lot of time trying to figure out if the person in their life is indeed a narcissist, or if they are just behaving narcissistically to a problematic degree. Frankly, it doesn't matter. What's important to realize is that if a person doesn't sincerely realize they have a problem, and isn't sincerely motivated to change, then they won't change. It doesn't matter if they are a narcissist, acting narcissistically, an alcoholic, a shopaholic, have an eating disorder or you name it. Staying in a toxic relationship hoping the other person will change while you are being dragged through hell is not healthy.

And that's the challenge with narcissists—they don't ever (sincerely) think that they have a problem. And if a person feels entitled and justified in all of their actions, then they are lacking the insight into how damaging their behavior is, as well as their responsibility in things. The first step in change is awareness that there is a problem, and unfortunately, the vast majority of narcissists never get to this first step. Even if they did, there are many additional steps after this one that they would need to take in order for their behavior to change because their problematic behavior is a deep-seated part of their personality. And trying to convince a person who doesn't see anything wrong with their actions that they need to change those actions will just annoy them and frustrate you.

Even if there was a treatment for narcissism, that doesn't mean that a narcissist will be motivated to use it or to actually change. After all, there are plenty of people who struggle with conditions that do have treatments such as alcoholics, anorexics, hoarders, compulsive gamblers or even those with medical issues that would only require them taking a pill or a shot, such as those with diabetes or high blood pressure who still aren't motivated to stick with the treatment, even if their life is on the line. I bring this up because it's important for you to realize how motivation to change is a big factor to change, and that change is always hard.

Most narcissists have a lack of empathy and remorse for their actions and feel entitled to behave in hurtful ways. Because of this, they rarely hit an emotional rock bottom and have the wake-up call that they are the problem. Often, they either hop from partner to partner, or the partner they are with continues to stay with them no matter how many times they lie, cheat, steal, manipulate, abuse, etc.

What if the narcissist is a parent/family member?

There are added challenges when distancing yourself from a family member who is narcissistic. It's common for other family members to get upset when a person starts drawing boundaries and not allowing this person with problematic behavior to have full and open access to their life. The common excuse given is, "But they are your mother/father/sibling/etc." And then this justification that "well, they are family" is spun around to shame, blame and guilt the person who wants to break free from the drama and dysfunction.

So prepare yourself for this.

You will most likely be made into the bad guy by other dysfunctional and enabling family members when you assert yourself and say that no, mom or dad can't move in with you and your family because they are addicts and spent their money on drugs and are now homeless, or that you want to file charges because mom stole your identity and opened up accounts in your name, or that no, you won't be giving your parents any more money because you can't afford to, or that no, it's not okay for your pedophile uncle to be around your children.

Enablers of abusive or toxic people, are also abusive and toxic, and it's okay (and often necessary) to distance yourself from them too. It's okay and healthy to have deal-breaker behavior or to distance yourself so that you feel safe and sane regardless of who the problematic person is.

If you do want to stay in contact with this person out of guilt, obligation, or for the sake of peace with other family members, you could consider going "low contact." This means you distance yourself and keep contact at a level with which you are comfortable.

Maybe you decide to fully cut contact, or maybe you decide to try something different. Maybe you would like to see them over Christmas, but that you'll fly there, and you'll stay for only three days. Or maybe you decide you want to stay in a hotel during those three days. Other people may argue with your boundaries, but this doesn't mean that you need to cave in and do things their way. They will either be okay with it, or they won't. If they aren't okay with your boundary, then it may negatively impact your relationship with them, but you do not have to defend your boundaries to anyone. You really don't. They might continually want to debate your decisions, but you can stand firm and say that you've made up your mind and there's nothing more to discuss—and to not bring it up again.

The boundaries you make aren't to punish the other person; they are to protect you. It's okay and healthy to not want to be around a person who is abusive or those who try and push you into keeping a dangerous or destructive person in your life.

How do I divorce (or break up with) a narcissist?

You go about divorcing a narcissist much like you go about knocking down a bee's nest. This means you have a plan of action in place where you are preparing for the worst but hoping for the best. Because leaving or divorcing a narcissist will trigger a narcissistic injury which will generally lead to narcissistic rage. Narcissists who are more on the mild end of the spectrum will most likely be bratty, difficult, entitled, snarky, and do things like refuse to sign papers, tie up the process in court, lie in court, hide money, or drain the bank accounts. At the more extreme end, narcissists can stalk and harass, launch smear campaigns, and even become dangerous and deadly. The more extreme situations have more in common with leaving a cult or escaping a hostage situation, and often require a safety plan, preparation, having the police do a civil standby, or leaving when the person is at work—with only what's most important.

Narcissists are the most dangerous when they feel they are losing control over their target and/or over the situation. So expect and plan for them to be on some of their worst behavior.

Here are some examples of how you can expect a narcissist to behave during a break-up. They may:

- Launch a smear campaign against you.

- Lie and manipulate.

- Paint themselves as the target of you.

- Move on quickly and post it all over social media.

218

- Have a cool or cruel level of indifference to the pain they are causing to you and the children.

- Try to manipulate your children by saying bad things about you.

- Say and do things to hurt your feelings, or to try to grind you down.

- Expect that others (including many of your friends, family, therapists, attorneys, judges, police) will not understand the severity of your situation and will instead treat your situation like it's a bad breakup.

- Be on their best behavior with promises of change.

- Be on their worst behavior and be potentially dangerous.

Here's also a list of things that I'd encourage you to expect from yourself. You will most likely:

- Think that you know the full truth of their bad behavior, when in reality you only know the tip of the iceberg.

- Be incredibly hurt and wonder if you could have done more to make things work.

- Find yourself trying to normalize their problematic behavior.

- Find that others try to normalize their bad behavior and who will offer no shortage of well-intended bad advice to push you into staying together.

- Be mad as hell (especially the more you read and understand about narcissism) once you start seeing how you were manipulated

- You might want to write them a letter or otherwise explain how much they are hurting you and/or the children in an attempt to get them to stop.

- Find yourself incredibly depressed, anxious, or suicidal at times.

Here are some ideas on how you could go about planning for these things:

-        Anticipate that the narcissist will launch a smear campaign against you. Keep a paper trail of everything that they are doing or saying. Ideally, take screen shots of social media (you can take pictures with your phone too). Have conversations through text, email, or a court appointed mediator.

-        Anticipate the coming lies and manipulation. This is what narcissists do. And when things don't go their way, or when they start losing control over their target or the situation, they will often throw out every trick in the book in order to regain control. It is a mistake to take a liar and a manipulator at face value…ever. Doing so will only set you up to fail.

-        Anticipate that they portray themselves as the victim. Odds are, they will accuse you of being a narcissistic, abusive, and manipulative, and will work to get others to side with them. This may include going to a therapist and getting a psychiatric evaluation to show that they aren't personality disordered and/or telling you that the therapist said that it sounded like you were the one with the problem. This will be confusing, crazy-making or infuriating (if you see the manipulation for what it is). And because they come across as convincing, they may have friends and family (maybe even some of your mutual friends, or your family) supporting them. This may make you wonder if you really are the problem, or if you are narcissistic or abusive and don't know it. If you start doubting your sanity and wondering if you could be abusive and not know it, ask yourself if someone else that you trusted saw what went on between you two, what would they say about this?

-        Anticipate that they could move on quickly and post it all over social media. Consider blocking them so you don't see what they are posting, and make it clear to your friends and family that you don't want to know what your ex is doing.

-        Anticipate them having a cool or cruel level of indifference to the pain they are causing you and the children. Realize that their hurtful behavior doesn't mean that you are bad, or the problem. Their hurtful behavior only shows that they are incapable of experiencing empathy and remorse at any deep level—and that a relationship with a person who doesn't experience these things will only ever cause you hurt and heartache. Let your children know that the way they are being treated is not their fault.

-        Anticipate them trying to manipulate people who know you (your friends and family, their friends and family, and even your children) by saying bad things about you, and encourage your friends, family, and especially your children to talk to you about anything negative that they might hear.

-        Anticipate that many others (including many of your friends, family, therapists, attorneys, judges, or police) will not understand the severity of your situation and will instead treat it like it's a bad breakup, or like you are over-reacting. Find some support groups online for narcissistic abuse, and turn to people who understand.

-        Anticipate for them being on their best behavior with promises of change, or to send you romantic or seemingly nice texts. Don't be fooled by this. It's very common for abusive people to say whatever they need to say in order to rope their target back into the relationship.

-        Anticipate that there will be a wide range of emotions, and that you will go from hating them to missing them. Realize that this is normal, and get a plan for how you will handle those moments when you are tempted to contact them.

How do I leave a narcissist in a safe way?

Creating a personalized safety plan involves brainstorming and planning for everything to be lined up in order to make leaving as smooth and as safe as possible. Elements of a safety plan often include: a safe place to go, copies of important papers, medications that would be needed, several changes of clothes, spare key to the vehicle, placement of the pets, and money. Ideally, all of these items would be hidden away from the abuser, so the target could leave immediately and not worry about being sabotaged in their efforts.

Here are the elements of a safety plan in more detail.

1. Develop a "safe word." A safe word is a word that you agree with a friend or family member ahead of time that lets them know you can't talk and are in danger. Make this word something that is unique, but nothing that would raise a red flag to anyone else. Something like "grey kitten" or "mocha." Agree on a word that you could work into a sentence like, "How is your new grey kitten?" or "I could really go for a mocha right now." Odds are this sentence will in no way shape or form be related to what you were just talking about, and it should alert the other person into knowing something is wrong. They need to know that you might not be able to answer any more questions, and that if you hang up, they need to call 911 and use a GPS locator on your phone to find your location, if possible.

2. Get copies (or ideally take originals) of all important papers. These would be copies of birth certificates (yours and the children's), social security cards, driver's licenses, auto insurance, auto registration, divorce papers, citizenship papers, immunization records, and anything else important.

3. Make extra sets of keys. Make extra sets of keys for your house and vehicles. Give a set to a friend, and keep a set somewhere hidden on the different vehicles in case you need to get out fast.

4. Pack a "go bag." Pack a bag of several sets of clothing and some shoes for the kids and yourself. Keep these bags someplace safe, like at a friend's house. Do not keep these bags where the abuser might find them. You do not want to alert them that you are leaving.

5. Store extra medications. If you or the kids are on medication, keep extras in your go bag. Make sure to also pack any medical supplies that might be needed, such as insulin syringes, blood tester, blood testing strips, asthma inhalers, etc. Check them periodically to make sure they aren't expired. And remember, a lot of medications need to be kept at room temperature or in the fridge.

6. Have a safe location. If you leave, you don't want the abuser to know where you are going. Line up a place to stay with friends, family, or a motel or hotel. Make sure that wherever you are going that they won't tell your abuser where you are. If you are in danger, or are concerned you might be, a domestic violence shelter may be an option.

7. Make sure to turn off the "Find my iPhone" or GPS feature on your phone. Your abuser can track you this way. If you aren't sure how to do this, google it or call your service provider ahead of time.

8. Don't hesitate to call the police. You may be struggling with whether or not to call the police out of fear that it might get them in trouble, or you think the abuse isn't "that bad" yet. If you or your children are being threatened, or if you feel like you might be in danger, call the police. It's better to err on the side of caution. Also, if there is a history of police reports that are filed, it can help to prove that there is a pattern of abusive behavior which can potentially help you later if you go to court.

9. Find alternative placement for your pets. If you are staying in an abusive relationship because of your pets (lots of people do), line up alternative placement with a friend or family member. Some domestic violence shelters may also be able to help you find temporary housing for your pets. I know that you want to protect your pets, but please remember if you don't protect yourself, you may not be around to protect them.

10. Only tell people that you trust. If you are leaving, or thinking of leaving, it's really important that you only tell people that you can trust. It's also a good idea to let them know that your former partner can be very manipulative, and regardless of what they say (that they need to get ahold of you because of some major issue with the kids, for example) that your trusted friend does not give them any information. Instead, they can take down the info and offer to pass it along if they happen to see you. I would also encourage you to have friends and family read more on the "hoovering" and "flying monkey" sections of this book, so they can also prepare for it.

Did they ever love me?

It's thought that narcissists don't have deep attachments to others—even to their children. This is, in part, why they are able to move on so quickly. They may have loved you in their own way, to their limited capacity, but we don't all have the same capacity for bonding, or bond to the same depth of feeling. So, their 100% might only be your 10%. Know that their behavior is a reflection of them and their capacity to love, not a reflection of you and how lovable you are.

How do I "gray rock" when they keep provoking me?

The best way to do this is to anticipate their behavior as much as possible, then to set up your interactions with them accordingly. When you anticipate their behavior, I think you will find that you become more emotionally detached from it, because you are seeing the immature antics and dysfunctional games for what they are. I find it helpful to view their behavior as adult temper-tantrums. And just like a child who doesn't get their way, narcissists will use every trick they have in order to get you to cave in. They will beg, plead, cry, threaten, scream, pout, say hurtful things, flatter, promise to be better; you name it. Don't cave in.

Once you fully see their behavior as the game that it is, going gray rock becomes much easier. With that said, going gray rock still takes practice. After all, it's hard to remain calm and non-reactive when someone is actively pushing your buttons. If you don't have to have contact with them, you are most likely best off blocking them, and possibly changing your email address, phone number, and/or physical address if their harassment doesn't stop. In addition, if at any point their behavior becomes threatening, you can always call the police. If you must keep some contact open because you have children with them, you can talk to your attorney about using a third party (website or apps) for communication if they need to discuss something about the child.

How can I prevent getting sucked back in again?

Thinking back to all the good times you had can be a slippery slope and can lead a person to minimize the bad times...which often results in reopening contact. If you have been in a relationship with anyone, even a narcissist, it's normal to miss certain things about them. It can be helpful to anticipate that nostalgia will set in from time-to-time so you don't get sucked back in.

One way to anticipate this is to make what I call your, "For When You Miss Him (or Her) List." In this list you write out in bullet point, easy-to-scan format of all the reasons you left this relationship or dynamic and why you need to keep this person out of your life. Then, when you start missing them, you can pull out this list and it will remind you of why you left.

In addition, it's also really helpful to build your circle of support and to focus on feeling good and having some fun. I totally understand that you might not feel like doing this, but it really will help you to move onto the next chapter in your life. Because the more you have going on in your life, the less you will miss them, and the more you are doing things that are fun and enjoyable with nice people, the more you won't ever want to go back to anything that is hurtful or harmful. I'm a big fan of the website meetup.com to find new things to do and to hopefully meet some nice, new people along the way. It's worldwide, free to join, and it's not a dating site.

What if they don't hoover me?

The main fear that I hear from people when their former partner doesn't hoover is that they fear that a lack of a hoover somehow means they were wrong about their former partner—that maybe this person wasn't a narcissist after all. And that maybe they broke up with this ideal (but very problematic) person before they gave them enough of a chance to change. If their behavior was abusive, the relationship wasn't healthy, and frankly, it needed to end. Holding onto hope that they might change is a recipe for disaster.

So while most narcissists hoover; some don't. Most narcissists hoover within the first few months, but it could be years or even decades before you hear from them again—so prepare yourself emotionally for this possibility. If you never hear from them again, this isn't a reflection of you or somehow indicate that you aren't lovable. It means that they have moved onto new supply, or that they realize that they can't get more supply from you.

And it's also very normal to be hurt and upset that they aren't hoovering you, as dysfunctional as that might sound. After all, it hurts like hell that they can move on so easily, while you are left feeling emotionally devastated.

What do I do if they are threatening to hurt themselves?

It is common for narcissists to try every angle in order to get their target to reopen communication, or to give them another chance. The more their target holds out, the more manipulative their behavior tends to become. It's not uncommon for them to threaten suicide (or to fake overdoses, or to lie about being in the hospital due to a suicide attempt) in order to push their target into reopening communication. This is generally a bluff designed to provoke their target into feeling pity. Regardless as to whether or not you feel their threats are sincere, this is still a highly manipulative and problematic thing for a person to do because it holds other people emotionally hostage. In addition, it shows just how unbalanced they really are.

What do you do in such a situation? Call your local emergency department (or 911 if you are in the US) and have them go check. There are three reasons for this. First, if the narcissist truly is suicidal, an emergency response team is best equipped to handle the situation. Second, if they truly are this desperate or upset, they can potentially become homicidal as well. You don't want to put yourself in harm's way. And third, if this threat isn't sincere, and they are using it as a manipulation, they will quickly learn that tactic doesn't work with you and that a response team will show up instead.

Is it normal to miss an abusive ex?

Yes, it is normal to miss an abusive ex. Odds are they weren't abusive 100% of the time. Perhaps the good times were really good, or perhaps they weren't even that good, but that you got crumbs of affection and attention from them, and it's hard to let go of that. Because their behavior wasn't hurtful or hateful all the time, it can be really confusing to determine what kind of person you were dealing with. This Dr. Jekyll and Mr. Hyde effect (and the resulting Stockholm Syndrome and trauma bonds) are confusing and can take a while for a person to see clearly for what they are, and for those bonds to break and for healthy thinking to return.

In addition, you were in a relationship with them. You shared part of your life with them. You bonded and created memories. If you are like most people who go through a relationship with

Dana Morningstar

an emotional manipulator, you made them a very big part of your world (if not your whole world) to the point where you put them first and everyone else second (and yourself last). These feelings and these bonds don't stop right away. Be patient with yourself as you move forward and heal.

Frankly, it's wise for you to plan on missing them at some point, so you are emotionally prepared for it if it does happen. This way, you won't be so upset with yourself for missing them or wanting to contact them. When these waves of nostalgia kick in, they can be a lot like the cravings that any addict experiences. And just like any other type of craving, you have to act on them. If you can ride the wave and find healthy and enjoyable ways to stay occupied, those cravings will pass. Being part of a support group can be really helpful, especially during this time.

How did I get involved in a relationship like this?

Well, there are lots of potential reasons for this, but at the core, emotional manipulators target people based on "supply" and they exploit people's vulnerabilities in order to get that supply. And since we all have vulnerabilities, we are all potential targets.

In addition, our vulnerabilities will change throughout our life. What made us vulnerable ten years ago is most likely not the same thing that makes us vulnerable today, or in a year from today. We will never get rid of all of our vulnerabilities, nor would we want to, as they aren't necessarily a bad thing. Being vulnerable is a core part of intimacy, and in many ways our vulnerabilities help us to be empathetic and to connect with others. It's when we don't know what our vulnerabilities are that they can be easily exploited and used against us.

Our main vulnerabilities tend to be ones that are either physical or emotional. These vulnerabilities may have been there from childhood, or they may be recent. For example, some vulner-abilities a person might have from childhood could be feeling unloved, unimportant, or craving stability. Some vulnerabilities a person might have later in life could be their age (especially if they are concerned about being single or having children), their income, low self-esteem, feeling lonely, feeling scared about money or being single, the loss of a spouse (through death or divorce), being new to town and not knowing anyone, starting a new job, or being a single parent.

If a person is feeling any of these ways, then they can be a prime target for an abusive relationship later on in life. If a person is feeling emotionally starved out, and unloved or unimportant then when they encounter love bombing, they will "eat it up" as it feels so amazing to finally be "fed." Whereas if a person is emotionally nourished, love bombing will feel as problematic as it is. When we are starved out or scared of being alone, it is easy to mistake charm for sincerity.

While being aware of all of our vulnerabilities is important, awareness of what manipulative and abusive behavior looks like in motion is perhaps the biggest key in steering clear of problematic people. For example, a lot of people got caught up with online scams (especially Nigerian prince scams or dating scams) about ten years ago. This is because these scams weren't widely known or discussed. Once people became aware of how online scammers operated, fewer people got caught up in them. Now that there is awareness, most people know not to give money or their bank info to strangers they meet online. Now it's not the target's fault they got caught up in these scams, just like it isn't our fault we got caught up with emotional manipula-tors. It is, however, worth taking time to examine your vulner-abilities to see if there are any that jump to the front of your mind. Ask yourself if these vulnerabilities have been driving your decisions about partners, friends and even careers.

When we are making decisions from a state of emotional

Dana Morningstar

scramble, we are not thinking clearly, but we don't realize it. What's even worse is that we often believe that we are thinking more clearly than ever before! (Yikes.) This is why it's a good idea not to make an important decision shortly after a major life change, such as moving across country, after a divorce, starting a new career, or after the death of a loved one.

Now don't get me wrong, I'm not blaming the target here. I'm not saying that any of this was your fault. It wasn't. Most people don't realize that there are manipulators out there with such a selfish and cruel indifference, that they mistakenly think others are just like them. It sometimes takes getting tangled up with an emotional manipulator to realize that not everyone has good intentions.

In addition to having emotional vulnerabilities we are unaware of, here are three other factors which often contribute to a person getting into a problematic or abusive relationship:

1. **We look for qualities that we wished our former partner had.** On the surface, this doesn't seem problematic—and it usually isn't, unless we've been in an abusive relationship, and then it really can be very problematic. The reason is that a person is trying to move away from the problematic character traits of their last partner, and this can often lead them crashing into someone with the same level of problematic behavior. What I mean is, that if our former partner was an overt narcissist, we will most likely seek out the polar opposite of that. But the polar opposite of an overt narcissist isn't a "healthy" person; the polar opposite is an overly charming and attentive covert narcissist. And so a person who is trying to avoid an outright abusive, selfish, inattentive, and cruel jerk is going to be a prime target for love bombing.

231

Interestingly enough, this can also be the case if the former partner was a covert narcissist. If a person dated a covert narcissist, they might now be very guarded around someone who is kind, considerate, attentive, and complimentary, and have a hard time telling the difference between love bombing and sincere (and appropriate) attention. If this is the case, they may find themselves (subconsciously) being attracted to an overt narcissist as it might feel safer to be with a person whose abusive behavior is more apparent. A person stuck in this cycle usually finds themselves having dated a quite a few narcissists, many of whom are back-to-back relationships. And that pattern might go something like: covert narcissist, then overt narcissist, then covert, then overt. They also may have made new friends during that time who are either covert or overt narcissists.

2. We look for qualities that feel comfortable. For example, if a person has had a series of relationships with controlling people (or had parents who were controlling), then that might feel comfortable to them, and dating a person who was less controlling might make them feel insecure and uncomfortable. This is often the case if a person has grown up in a troubled or abusive home, where controlling behavior was often confused with caring behavior, and abuse of any kind seemed normal. A person who finds themselves in this type of repeating pattern might use the justification that "things could always be worse." They compare what they are experiencing to what they've experienced in the past, not realizing that abuse is abuse, and while it could be worse, that doesn't make what's happening now tolerable.

3. We look for partners based off of our own level of dysfunction. If we have some sort of addiction, vice, or problematic behavior that we don't want to stop, then odds are we aren't going to be looking for a partner (or a healthy relationship) but more of a co-conspirator or enabler. So for example, if we have a drinking problem, then we will be attracted to someone who drinks too, or we'll be attracted to someone who will put up with (enable) our drinking.

4. We are looking for someone else's love to fix us. It's very common (and understandable) for a person to get out of an abusive relationship and be left feeling broken beyond repair. They may be looking to others to love them enough that all those broken pieces become whole again. This isn't healthy, it's codependent. It may work in the short term, but only as long as that person stays around. If they leave or get hit by a bus, then we are back at square one feeling empty and unloved. Many people don't realize that it's not healthy to look to others to "complete" us. Dysfunctional childhoods, the media, toxic ideology and views of religion, and pretty much most of the main stream ideas of love set up a person to get into (and stay in) codependent and dysfunctional relationships and friendships. By the time most of us reach dating age, we have been primed to confuse love bombing with love, intensity with sincerity, control with caring, and codependency with commitment. Frankly, it's a miracle that anyone doesn't experience at least one relationship or friendship with an emotional manipulator considering all the toxic messages we've been given over the years.

How can I stop attracting narcissists?

We all attract a wide range of people, and we don't have that much control over whom we attract. What's more important, and what we do have control over, is who we are attracted to and how long we keep problematic people in our lives.

With that said, there are certain things that are a turnoff to narcissists, such as solid boundaries, assertive communication, and healthy self-esteem. Even if a narcissist slips under your radar and into your life, holding to your solid boundaries of how you expect to be treated and knowing your deal breakers for how you will not be treated will get them out a lot sooner than later.

I want to bring up a quick side note about boundaries, because

I see this a lot (and I did this too for many years). Having solid boundaries doesn't mean yelling, screaming, begging, pleading, threatening, going to therapy, and overall continually trying to fix a problematic relationship (or other person). Having solid boundaries means having deal-breaker behavior and then actually walking away if things don't change. In order to keep narcissists and other emotional manipulators out of our lives, we need to be okay with actually keeping them out of our lives—not keeping them in our lives and forever trying to fix them or trying to make things work.

How do I handle all of this intense anger that I have?

It's normal to have a mix of emotions after getting out of an abusive relationship, and anger is one of those emotions with which many people struggle. Your anger is understandable, and as you learn more about abusive behavior, you will understand what happened and how someone was able to slowly gain power and control over you. It's appropriate and normal to be very angry about being manipulated, used, and abused and that your feelings, sanity and safety were exploited and eroded, all for their selfish reasons. And it's normal and understandable to feel even more angry when other people minimize, invalidate, argue about or deny what happened to you—especially if these people are friends, family, or someone you reached out to for clarity and healing like a therapist, a psychologist, or a religious counselor.

This anger can be overwhelming, so much so that you might avoid other people altogether, because all you can think about is the trauma you went through, and those around you don't want to hear about it or they want to invalidate your feelings.

Here are some ideas for working through anger after an abusive relationship:

-       Realize that feeling this level of anger is healthy

and appropriate for how you were treated (even though your level of anger and rage might feel overwhelming).

-        Make the decision that even though this anger is healthy, appropriate, and an important stage in healing, you are not going to let anger consume you or destroy your life.

-        Pay special attention to what you are feeding your brain. You may want to feed your brain information that helps to keep you calm, peaceful, and gives you a sense of security and safety. Or if you are having a hard time expressing your anger (which is also normal), then you may find it helpful to watch movies or listen to music that let you get in touch with your anger.

-        Keep a journal.

-        Talk to other people in a support group.

-        Use physical activity to burn off some of the anxious energy.

-        Be around people who support you (and who don't try to convince others about what happened).

-        Realize that the abusive person is manipulative, and that the other people who support them are the "new supply" have also been unknowingly manipulated.

-        Try to harness as much of that anger energy as possible and think of it as rocket fuel that you can use to build a great life for yourself.

-        Make continual efforts when you feel anger to

acknowledge that this is how you feel, and to reassure yourself that it's okay to feel this way.

-       Sit with it and explore it, or if that is too uncomfortable or overwhelming, channel it into something positive such as cleaning out your closet, going for a walk/ run, yelling and saying all the things you want to say to the manipulator out loud while hitting a pillow.

-       Make affirmations.

-       Meditate. Take a few moments throughout the day to ground yourself and be in the present moment.

-       Find a mantra. Choose a short phrase that helps remind you of the direction that you want to head. Some examples might be, "The best revenge is a good life," or "I can do this," or "I will get through this," or "I am worthy of being treated with dignity and respect."

-       Practice Gratitude. Gratitude is perhaps the most effective and most instantaneous tool against the venom of anger. Being grateful for the things that are working well in your life, or things that you appreciate does not mean that you aren't angry about what happened to you. It simply means that you choose not to be blinded by that anger or to let it consume your every moment of every day. You can experience a wide mix of emotions. Even though your primary emotions may be anger, rage, and hurt, you can still experience gratitude, contentment, peace, calm, and even happiness and joy.

Chapter 8: Finding the Right Support Group and Therapist

There are lots of different support groups out there, and currently, there are many more online support groups than in-person groups for narcissistic abuse. If privacy is even a small concern, and you want to join an online group, please, please, please do so under a fake name (one that you've never used before) with a picture that is either not you or that you haven't used before online. The reason is that someone can do a google search for the screen name you've used, as well as the picture that you've used online and any other site that you've used those pictures or that name will show in the search results. Even with taking these steps, no support group can 100% guarantee your privacy. People can get in there and take screenshots or pass things around on the internet. I'm not saying any of this to scare you; I'm saying this to prepare you so you can use a healthy degree of caution with what you post.

Keeping your identity private

Regardless of what type of group you join on Facebook, you may want to consider changing your group and profile settings to hide this information if you feel that potentially problematic or pot-stirring people are watching what you are doing. You can do this in your Facebook settings that can be found within your profile page.

If you don't want anyone knowing that you are in a group on narcissistic abuse, you may want to do one of the following:

-        Join a blog/website-based group (here is a link to

mine: www.thriveafterabuse.com/forum)

-        Join a "secret" group on Facebook (although like I mentioned before, no online is 100% private unless you join under a fake name).

-        Create an alternate Facebook profile in order to protect your privacy. You would do this by setting up another email, then joining Facebook with a fake (but still real-sounding name). If you go this route, make sure that you keep this profile as secret as possible. Only use it to participate in support groups. Don't "friend" people outside of the support groups. Especially don't friend your family or friends, as this will show up in their news feed. If someone is watching your (or their) account, they will connect the dots pretty quickly and realize that you've created an alternate profile.

-        Avoid sharing specific details about your situation or location online until appropriate levels of trust have been developed in order to maintain as much privacy as possible.

Ways to stay safe in groups

When people join a support group, they often find themselves very relieved that others understand where they are coming from, that this isn't all in their head, and that what they have been experiencing really is highly problematic. Because they feel so understood, they are often quick to let their guard down and to assume that everyone who has been through narcissistic abuse is like them.

This is not the case.

It's important to have healthy boundaries wherever you go, even in support groups. If someone starts messaging you, or has requests that make you feel uncomfortable, it's healthy and appropriate to hold your boundary with them. You don't need to message someone back or meet with them if you are uncomfortable. This isn't being rude (although it may feel that way); this is setting a boundary. Let me repeat, if you feel something is "off" with someone, odds are it is because something is "off." Tell one of the group administrators so that they can (at a minimum) keep an eye on this person, or remove them from the group if need be.

If you do decide to meet up with people you've met through online support groups, make sure it is in a public place, and make sure you don't give out your address. Do not stay the night at their house, and do not let them stay the night at your house—even if they (or you) are driving several hours to meet them. Do not meet them at their house, or at any public location where there aren't others around. Do not loan them money. Do not give them money. I can't stress this enough: healthy boundaries must always be in place at all times.

Consider joining a few in order to find some that resonate with you. Every group has its own rules and its own dynamic.

There are many support groups online that are free, and that run around the clock. Here is a link to mine: www.thriveafterabuse.com/forum

Another issue that tends to be a common struggle with online groups (especially Facebook groups) is that they are often very active, and a person may get hundreds of responses to their post, as well as get notified of dozens of new posts every day. This can be very overwhelming, and the heaviness of this topic can be too much at times. If you start feeling this way, consider turning off the notifications from your Facebook groups. This way you won't get any more of the group notifications, and then you can go there whenever.

Understanding Online Support Groups That Are on Websites

There are two main types of online support groups: forums and Facebook groups.

A forum, or "open" group is a group on a blog or website.

Pros: You can create your own user name, and your identity is not openly tied to the account. So even though anyone can read what you are posting, they don't openly have access to your name or other personal details, unless you for some reason you make them known (which, again, I highly recommend that you don't.)

Cons: Anyone who goes to that website can see what you are posting.

Potential Safety Concerns: Consider selecting a user name that is vague and protects your real identity. For example, a person could use names like "NextChapter," "JaneDoe" or "JohnDoe."

A "closed" forum on a website

A closed forum on a website is often a hidden or restricted access portion of an open group. Usually closed forums are for paying members (but not always).

Pros: Only those who have access to that section of the group can see what you are posting.

Cons: If people are only posting in closed areas, then new members who haven't joined those areas yet won't be able to give or get as much feedback on their posts as they might like.

Potential Safety Concerns: The same concerns regarding a user name as an open website group.

Understanding Facebook Groups

"Open" Facebook groups

Open groups on Facebook are open to everyone on Facebook. There is no privacy, and anyone can see what you are posting.

Pros: This type of group format allows for a wide variety of people to ask and answer questions.

Cons: Anyone on Facebook can read the posts and anyone can join.

Safety Concerns: Since anyone can get in, internet trolls and bullies tend to flock to these kinds of groups, not to mention that anyone on Facebook can see what you are posting. This can be potentially embarrassing and put someone at risk for online (or offline) harassment or stalking.

"Closed" Facebook Groups

You can find these groups by doing a search on Facebook for a specific topic. Only other members of the Facebook group can see what you are posting.

Pros: There is more privacy as compared to an open group.

Cons: Since the group is on Facebook, your Facebook profile is associated with it. Depending on your privacy settings, people in the group will know your name and anything else you have on your Facebook profile.

Potential Safety Concerns: You will need to check (or change) your privacy settings to make sure that your other Facebook friends can't see what groups you are in.

"Private" Facebook groups

These groups are invitation only, and cannot be seen if someone is searching for them.

Pros: These groups offer the maximum amount of privacy allowed on Facebook. No one outside of the group can see that you are a member of the group, nor can they request to join. They must be directly invited to join these groups.

Cons: Secret groups do not show up if you search for them, so it makes finding one to join very difficult. And the same as open or closed groups; since the group is on Facebook, your Facebook profile is associated with it. Depending on your privacy settings, people in the group will know your name and anything else you have on your Facebook profile.

Potential Safety Concerns: At any time, Facebook may change its policies about how they promote groups and who can see what, so privacy isn't guaranteed.

Finding the Right Therapist

A lot of people tend to go with a therapist that their insurance covers, or who has an office closest to their home. However, all therapists (like any other professional) are not created equal, and finding the right fit is crucial. Finding the right therapist, like finding the right professional in any area, whether it be a financial planner, a Realtor, a landscaper, a doctor, an attorney, etc. can be a challenge, and sometimes you may have to go to several before you find a good fit.

It's really important that a therapist (and especially spiritual leaders) don't have their own self-esteem needs or belief systems wrapped up in "saving" your relationship, and instead are supportive of your doing what you need to do in order to stay safe and sane.

While it may seem counter-intuitive, a big red flag to look for is if a therapist or spiritual counselor takes great pride in their ability to keep couples together. While improved communication between two people can be a great thing, it's not the core issue of an abusive relationship—and to have it treated as such is not only incredibly damaging and dangerous to the person in the relationship, but it can be incredibly revictimizing and traumatizing. You shouldn't have to improve your communication, be more understanding, or be more attentive or sexual to avoid being abused. And frankly, it wouldn't work anyway, because the abuse isn't due to anything you are (or are not) doing.

Before you set up an appointment, ask the therapist a few questions on the phone to see if they'd be a good fit for you and your situation, such as:

-        Do they have experience working with clients who have been in emotionally and psychologically abusive relationships?

-        Are they familiar with PTSD and how it can be caused by verbally and emotionally abusive relationships?

-        What is their view of divorce?

-        Are they wanting you to immediately participate in couple's counseling with an abusive (or chronically cheating) partner? (If so, watch out—because the odds of the abusive person manipulating the therapist into making their behavior a communication or relationship issue is really high.)

During and after the first session, check in with yourself to see how you feel. If you are experiencing some anxiety, hyper-vigilance, and distrust, this might be normal given what you've been through, but try to sort out how you feel about the session as well as how you feel about the connection you have (or don't have) with the therapist.

Some questions that you may want to ask yourself are:

- Do you feel comfortable with this therapist?

- Do you feel validated?

- Do you feel believed?

So how do you know when you've found a good therapist? You'll know when you find one with whom you feel comfortable, one who can educate and empower you about the dynamics of an abusive relationship, and one who can brainstorm strategies with you on how to move forward and heal.

Chapter 9: How Can I Help Someone in an Abusive Relationship?

Every month I have several dozen people contact me wanting to know what they can do to help a loved one who is in an abusive relationship. They are usually struggling with feelings of grief, fear, depression, anxiety, emotional exhaustion, and helplessness as they watch their loved one sink further into the clutches of a manipulative and abusive person.

Trying to help someone out of an abusive relationship is a lot like trying to help someone leave a cult. You have a similar dynamic of an intense "leader" and a highly manipulated target who has been brainwashed with many faulty beliefs—in this case specifically about what love and commitment are. The added challenge is that not only are a lot of these skewed beliefs coming from the abusive person, but from society as well—especially if they have surrounded themselves with others that have a "commitment at all costs" mindset. All of these factors can make trying to help a loved one very challenging, and please know that there is no magic phrase or one thing that you can do to get them to see things clearly. However, there are some things you can expect, and some things that you can do which can help them to see the situation clearly a lot sooner:

- **Keep communication open.** Let them know that you are there to talk, or to listen—whatever they need. If they are not willing to leave, or if they leave and then continue to go back, let them know that you care about them, and try to come from a place of being nonjudgmental, and supportive.

- **Try to understand where they are coming from emotionally.** Whenever any of us do something that we

246

feel is problematic, we tend to either minimize what we are doing, or we hide it. For example, if a person has an eating disorder or an addiction, they will hide the problem until things get so bad they are forced to reach out. If their reaching out results in being shamed ("How could you let this happen?" or "What is wrong with you?" or "You need to stop doing that!"), then most people shut down and don't get the help they need. Abusive relationships are no different. When a person is in one, they are most likely feeling a mix of confusion and distress, as well as shame and embarrassment for staying and for how they are being treated. However, if you join in on criticizing them or their relationship, they will most likely become defensive and distance themselves from you.

- Try to validate how they feel, and let them know that they aren't causing the abuse, and that they can't make the person stop abusing them either. If you feel at a loss for what to say or do, ask them how you can best support them during this time. They may tell you that they just need someone to listen, or that they are overwhelmed with how to go about leaving. Let them take the lead with what they need.

- **Give them resources.** There are lots of YouTube videos and blog articles out there on this topic that you can find by googling "narcissistic abuse." Other terms you might want to tell them to look up are "projection," "gaslighting," and "love bombing." You may also want to give them a link to an online support group and encourage them to see if this might help give them the clarity or validation they are seeking. This allows them to explore what's going on in a way that they don't feel judged or pressured, as well as it lets them explore this topic at their own pace. Support groups can be especially validating as it's often a lot easier to see issues in our own lives through hearing the stories of others.

- **Prepare yourself emotionally for them to go back.** Understand that both manipulative and abusive behavior is confusing behavior, and that because of this (as well as other reasons) most people go back on average seven times before the abusive person's behavior gets so undeniably bad that they leave for good. It can be absolutely infuriating and crazy-making to watch a loved one go back time and time again—especially if you are going to great lengths physically, emotionally, and financially to help them get away. You may get to the point where you want to throw your hands up in the air, or you may want to cut off contact with them because it's too draining for you—especially if they continue to go back. If you are finding yourself heavily invested in the outcome of whether or not they stay (and it's hard not to), this is a sign to take a few steps back. You will need to try to walk the line of supporting them while at the same time emotionally detaching from the outcome as much as possible so that you don't sink yourself trying to save them. I know that may sound harsh, and I for sure don't mean it to be, but please realize that helping a person leave can be a lot like running a marathon (and not a sprint), and you'll have to learn to pace yourself so you don't burn out. Also, please know that at the end of the day, they can only save themselves. This can be a devastating realization to grasp, but it's not healthy for you if you are sinking yourself to save them.

- **Continually reinforce that you care.** Continually remind them that you love and support them with whatever decision they make. This may sound like terrible advice if they are with a destructive or dangerous person, but at the end of the day, the choice is ultimately theirs, and they will most likely hang onto hope for quite a while that this person will eventually change and that this relationship can be saved. Letting them know that you support them regardless if they stay or leave will help to soften their defensiveness about their situation, which can help them to feel more comfortable with opening up to you. Remember, keeping communication open and keeping a good relationship with them are your main tools in getting through to them.

- **Be patient.** People in an abusive relationship are people who have been and are being majorly manipulated at every turn. When a person is being manipulated, they feel constant confusion. In an attempt to gain clarity, they often feel the need to talk (a lot) about what happened. This need to continually rehash events can go on for years after the relationship is over and is often misidentified (even by many professionals) as them dwelling on the past. This rehashing is part of a complex post-traumatic stress disordered response (C-PTSD), and is a normal response to an abnormal situation. It is the brain's way of putting the pieces together and trying to make logical sense out of an illogical situation so that it can figure out what happened, so that it doesn't happen again.

- This rehashing can be exhausting and frustrating for friends, family, and even therapists, and can lead to well-intentioned but unhelpful advice such as "get over it," "move on," "let it go," or even, "let's talk about something different." Those kinds of responses can feel very minimizing and silencing. Remember, this person has already been minimized and silenced by their abusive partner; they need to find their voice again and feel heard now.

- Remember, this isn't just a bad breakup, it has more to do with leaving a cult or escaping a hostage situation. When a person's sense of reality is manipulated, they often feel as if they've been raped emotionally and psychologically. It is incredibly violating and takes time to process. Perhaps the most helpful thing is to say, "I'm sorry this happened to you," or "I can see why you'd be so angry/hurt/confused." If you are feeling burned out, or like they need more help then what you feel like you can offer, referring them to a support group can really help. This way they can go through that rehashing process with others who are going through it too.

- **Avoid criticizing their partner or their relationship.** They may come to you, upset with what's going on and how they are being abused or cheated on…again. And you may find yourself enraged and telling them that their partner is abusive or a jerk, or that their relationship is abusive. If they aren't ready to leave, then saying things like this will often cause them to either become defensive of their partner or of the relationship, or feel a tremendous amount of shame, and they will most likely start justifying what's going on—which oftentimes leads them into talking themselves into staying.

- **Avoid arguing with their reality.** It can take years for a person to come to terms with the fact that their relationship was abusive. They might describe their partner as someone who yells, screams, belittles, calls them names, cusses, pushes, hits, cheats, lies, steals, is controlling, etc., but they might not see this as abusive, because in their mind it's only abuse or a problem if they are being hit on a regular basis, or if they can no longer tolerate it. It can be helpful to point out that these are all abusive behaviors, so that the person can at least be validated in that what they are experiencing is in fact beyond the realm of normal relationship issues, but if they start getting defensive about what they are experiencing, take this as a sign to back down a bit (because if you don't, they might shut down and stop communicating with you about what's happening). The same goes if they are describing their relationship as abusive; don't downplay it just because it doesn't match your understanding of what abuse is. Many people are only familiar with extreme physical abuse as being problematic and downplay other forms of abuse. Make no mistake; all forms of abuse cause harm. Just because you can't see the bruises, doesn't mean that damage hasn't been done.

- **It can be helpful to "mirror" their language**. If a person describes their relationship as abusive, then follow their lead and use the word abusive. If they use the word "toxic" then use the word "toxic." If they use the word "manipulative" then use the word "manipulative." If they aren't comfortable calling what they went through "abuse," don't force them to call it "abuse." Let them connect the dots in their own time, and define their own reality. Again, giving them resources such as links to videos, articles, books or support groups can help, as they will most likely gain a lot of clarity from hearing the experiences of others.

- **Avoid criticizing them for staying (or asking them why they didn't leave sooner).** Hindsight is always 20/20, and no one gets themselves into a bad situation intentionally. Additionally, leaving an abusive relationship generally isn't easy to do—on any level. Outside of ongoing manipulation, there are usually other factors at play: finances are often combined, children are used as pawns, intimidation, fear, religion, hope, and promises of change are also often used for control, the target is usually isolated from friends and family, and their self-esteem is ground down. Any one of these things makes leaving incredibly difficult.

- **Validate them.** Understand that they were targeted, manipulated, and taken advantage of, and that their anger is righteous anger. After all, you'd be really mad too, if someone pretended to be your ideal partner, then slowly revealed that they were an abusive monster or was living a double life. Especially if all the while friends, family, even therapists or spiritual leaders tried to convince you to stay and work on your part in things, and after years of doing this, and finally jumping ship when you couldn't handle it anymore--to then be asked why you stayed for so long is infuriating.

- As a member of my support group once beautifully and appropriately said, "Anger is a stage in healing, and one that needs to be respected." Anger is a part of them reclaiming their voice, their emotions, and their power and control over their life.

- **Know your limits.** Staying cool, calm, and collected while watching someone be manipulated, lied to, or abused can be frustrating, exhausting, and infuriating. This can (and often does) burn out friends, family, mental health professionals, and even other survivors. It's good for you to know your limits and encourage them to find several online support groups so that they can do a lot of their venting and gathering clarity and validation there.

- **Don't encourage them to get out there and start dating again.** It generally takes a person several years before they are even close to being ready to trust people (or their judgment about people) again, let alone date. They have had their boundaries eroded, and most likely have some major self-esteem issues to overcome. And because of this, they are incredibly vulnerable, and it is a mistake to be dating when a person is vulnerable, because the odds of them getting into another abusive relationship are really high. Instead, encourage them to make peace with where they are, to become more active in hobbies or with good people whom they've known for a while, and realize that they will heal in their own time frame, and that's okay.

Chapter 10: Strategies to Help You Move Forward

Moving forward doesn't mean "getting over" what happened to you, or even getting back to where you were. It means creating a new and empowering vision for this next chapter in your life. …And stepping into this new future can happen now, and it starts with taking small steps in the direction that you want to head on a regular basis.

While you may find yourself feeling profoundly broken or scared that you will never love or trust again, please know that the way you feel is normal and understandable given what you've been through. Also know that the pain won't always be this intense, and that many of your best days are still ahead of you. As the saying goes, "If you find yourself walking through hell, keep walking." Move in the direction that is the most empowering and gives you the most peace. You can do this.

Reclaiming Your Power and Control

You might find yourself struggling with how to handle all of the anger, rage, depression, anxiety, and overwhelm that tends to come along with moving forward. Here are some of the biggest things that helped me, that I hope will help you too:

- **Release the hope of ever getting closure from them**. You most likely really want to write them a letter or meet up with them and let them know how much they hurt you or how awful they really are. You may think that in doing this, you will get closure. You won't. One of two things happens instead: They either blame you for all the abuse, or they either pretend to be sorry—that they don't deserve you, or that they are tired of hurting you. Either way, reopening contact with them will open you up to more abuse. Because while you may have gotten what seems like a sincere apology or acknowledgment

254

of wrong doing, that's not what it is. It's more manipulation to either make you feel bad for leaving (thinking that maybe now they finally get it and that they will go on to have this happy, healthy relationship with the next person because you just gave up too soon), or it's designed to get you to feel sorry for them, which leaves the door open for them to come back—which they will generally do claiming that they need to talk, or need a friend, or miss you, or what not. You will never get honesty, truth, or respect from a dishonest, lying abuser. Remember that.

- **Give yourself closure.** Write that letter letting them know how you feel, and then gather up all the items in your home that remind you of them that you are wanting to eliminate. Call some friends and have a closure ceremony, or have it by yourself. Start a fire in a fire pit or in a fireplace and burn these things, as a symbolic way of closing the door on that chapter of your life.

- **Decide right now that you are not going to let this ruin your life.** I found that the ending of an abusive relationship can be so overwhelming and confusing that it helps to keep things as simple as possible. I embraced four mindsets which really helped to guide my thinking into a positive and powerful direction. Those mindsets are:

- I made the decision to not end my life over this.

- I made the decision to not let this ruin my life.

- I made the decision to take what happened to me and

use it for my highest and greatest good.

- I made the decision to take what happened to me and use it for the highest and greatest good for others.

What these four mindsets look like in motion will depend on you, should you choose to embrace them. In addition, I made the very conscious decision to not stay bitter or hateful—that I was going to allow myself to feel that way for a while, but that I wasn't going to stay there. I decided that I was going to try and bring as much light and love into the world as possible, in big and small ways every single day. I guess it was my way of feeling like I was winning over the dark vortex that is abuse.

- **Rein in your thinking.** Odds are your thoughts are probably all over the place, ranging from feeling optimistic, to feeling revicitimized, overwhelmed, suicidal, and many emotions in between. You can even out

Дана Morningstar

some of these highs and lows of this emotional roller coaster by taking certain options off the table. Many people struggle with feeling suicidal after the end of an abusive relationship. I strongly encourage you to take the option of suicide off the table. Don't even let your mind go there. If your mind does keep going there, please reach out to a suicide hotline, a doctor, or call your local emergency number for help.

- **You don't need to wait until you are fully healed to start enjoying your life again.** I know that it might feel like you need to be healed before you can get out there and enjoy life again, but healing actually works the opposite way: healing doesn't lead to happiness, it's happiness that leads to healing. Taking time for gratitude and enjoying the little things doesn't mean that you are somehow okay with what happened to you or that you aren't in pain. It just means that trauma and enjoyment can coexist at the same time, and that you aren't going to let this trauma sink you. A great way to get back out into life and to meet new friends and try new things is through the website www.meetup.com. It's not a dating site; it's for people who are looking to have fun, try new things, and meet new people. I encourage people to join a few dozen meetup groups. You don't have to go to every event, and it will give you options of things to do.

- **Develop a mantra.** A mantra is a word or phrase that helps to continually remind you of the direction in which you want to head. During the aftermath of an abusive relationship, a mantra can be a light in the emotional fog. As you move forward in your healing (and in life in general) the words and phrases that res-onate with you as a mantra will grow and change with

257

you. Some examples of a mantra are, "Peace." or "I can do this." or "Be here now." When I was feeling incredible amounts of rage, my mantra was "The best revenge is a good life." Having a mantra felt like a floating piece of debris that I could grab onto during the emotional storms that would often kick up and threaten to pull me under. I could then harness and transmute all of that rage-filled energy into something positive that would serve to bring my mantra into being. So for example, when I was upset, I'd tell myself, "The best revenge is a good life," and I'd then go get busy on bringing that "good life" into being. Some of the ways I did this was organizing a junk drawer, cleaning out my closet, washing my car, pulling weeds, doing sit ups, eating healthy food, calling a friend, painting my nails, playing with my dog, watching a comedy, or going for a long walk.

- **Feed your brain.** If you are feeling anxious, depressed, scared, overwhelmed, fearful, or distrusting, it can be helpful to be aware and selective about what you are exposing yourself to. So this may not be the best time to watch TV shows or movies or that are dramatic, violent, or romantic, or listening to music that makes you feel angry, sad, or nostalgic. You may find more relief from watching comedies, cartoons, documentaries about topics that you don't find upsetting, or empowerment or motivational talks (such as TED talks).

- **Practice picking up and putting down your emotions.** You may feel stuck in anger or obsessing about what happened. When we undergo a trauma of any kind, it's normal and natural for our brain to become obsessive about figuring out what happened and why, so that it can figure out what it needs to do in order for us to stay safe next time. And much like a complex computer, our brain runs through all the different experiences and situations, pulling them apart, examining them, and then putting them back together. It takes time for our brain to collect and combine everything in a way that makes sense, as well as to form a new understanding about what happened. The result of all this obsessing and rehashing is called "integration." During this time it's normal to feel stuck in this trauma. You might feel as if you are carrying a fifty-pound weight on your back all day, every day, but it also feels like you can't set it down either. Because if you set it down and allow yourself to enjoy life, that means you are somehow okay with what happened to you. This does not have to be the case.

- I encourage you to take time every day to practice releasing the clutches of obsessive thinking. What has helped me and many others is to visualize this trauma as only a fifty-pound weight that you are carrying on your back in a backpack. Now visualize taking off that backpack and placing it in the corner, or in the backseat of your car, or in a place you know where it is and where you can glance over at it as many times as you want to. Allow yourself to do something for the next ten minutes or two hours, or however long feels comfortable, such as watching a comedy, or funny animal videos on YouTube, or listening to a TED talk. And while you do this, if the old thoughts resurface, remind yourself that right now you are giving your brain a break and you will go back to thinking those thoughts (picking up that backpack) once the show is over. It's okay to give yourself a break; all of "this" will be there in an hour. In this way, you release the vice grip your brain has on your thinking and emotions, which can help you to shift out of feeling stuck and move back into living life.

- **Rearrange (or replace) furniture or other household items.** There is a lot to be said for changing up the energy or flow in an environment, especially after something traumatic has happened. If you have to stay in your former house where the abuse occurred, you may find it tremendously helpful to reclaim the space as your own. You could do this by rearranging the furniture, getting rid of certain items that are especially emotionally charged, getting some new pieces of furniture, hanging up new art work, painting the walls, and so on. You might be surprised by how helpful it can be to change your space and reclaim it as your own.

- **Get rid of "triggering" objects.** If you have objects or clothing that reminds you of them, consider selling, donating, or throwing out these things. If you cannot get rid of them yet, perhaps consider packing them up and keeping them out of sight.

- **Get a makeover.** Getting a different hairstyle, coloring your hair, painting your nails, getting some new clothes can feel very transformative—like you are shedding an old skin. If someone had told me this, I'm not sure I would have believed them, but seriously, you might be surprised as to how transformative it can feel to simply paint your toenails a different color. This is especially the case if your appearance was being dictated by the narcissist. If they didn't like your wearing makeup, put on some makeup. If they didn't like you with blonde hair, consider some blonde highlights. Taking charge and making some small decisions in your life can go a long way to reclaim your power and control over yourself and your life. You make the decisions in your life now—there is no one there to criticize you or to put down your decisions. The other added benefit to changing up your appearance, is that it can also serve as a very physical reminder of change, a reminder that you are moving forward into this next chapter in your life.

- **Surround yourself with people who "get it" and who support you.** Please don't try to get an abusive person to see how they are being abusive, or get friends and family to see how they are enabling bad behavior or invalidating you. To do so is not only an exercise in crazy-making, but it's a battle that you really don't need to spend time and energy fighting. Instead, I strongly encourage you to surround yourself with supportive people. Support groups or a good therapist can be really, really helpful during this time.

- **Create a written or video journal.** You are healing in small ways every single day, and small changes can be difficult to recognize, as well as remember. Writing down or videoing all your small wins can help you see the progress you are making. And when you look back on your journal in six months from now, I think you'll find how amazed you are with how far you've come— and you'll probably also see how much strength you had (that you didn't initially see) during those first few months when the relationship ended.

- **Reframe your understanding of the pain.** The one thing I did that gave me the most peace, was to reframe how I was interpreting my emotional pain. Instead of letting the pain completely overwhelm me and make me bitter and angry, I tried to remind myself that the pain is there to serve a purpose. Just like when we touch a hot stove, the purpose of that pain is to deliver the message of "Don't touch this (or any other) hot stove because doing so will hurt you." The purpose of the emotional pain I was in had a very similar message:

"Don't go near this person (or anyone who treats you like them)—doing so will hurt you." When I changed my relationship with my pain, and realized it was there to help keep me safe, it was no longer my enemy and something from which I needed to run. Remember, love doesn't hurt. It's being treated with a lack of love that hurts, and this pain that you are feeling is a reminder to stay away from people who hurt you.

- **Acknowledge your small wins.** Maybe you didn't cry today, or maybe you did cry for the first time. Maybe you got out of bed and took a shower. Maybe you cooked yourself a nice meal. Maybe you had some fun. Congratulating yourself for these small wins is so vitally important, because it's through these small wins that we reclaim our lives.

You are not alone. You are not crazy. You can heal from this.

I wish you light and love on this next chapter in your life, and I sincerely hope that you are able to move into all the health, healing, and happiness possible. …And a lot is possible. You can do this.

(((HUGS)))

Dana

About the Author

My name is Dana Morningstar, and my formal background is in education, domestic violence awareness and prevention, crisis intervention, trauma response, and psychiatric nursing. Over the past twenty years, I've had extensive experience working with both victims of abuse and abusers, as well as with those with a wide range of mental health challenges including a variety of trauma, crisis, mental illness, and personality disorders. However, I started down this road of talking about narcissistic abuse by trying to understand several of my own "problematic" relationships and friendships that I've had in my life. The more that came into focus, the more I felt compelled to share my aha moments with others in hopes that perhaps some of my hard-won lessons could help them get the clarity and validation they were seeking. I have since combined both my personal and professional experience into forming ThriveAfterAbuse.com, a website, podcast, and YouTube channel that is designed to help educate and empower those who are going through or who have been through abuse of any kind.

However, while the fall-out from abusive behavior often leads to tremendous amounts of devastation and destruction, it's with destruction that comes the ability for transformation. And in my journey, I've had the pleasure of coming across so many others who were on the same path looking for clarity and healing, as well as looking to share their experiences and insights. I receive many emails every day from people seeking support for themselves, their clients, or those they help teach or advise including therapists, domestic violence agencies, college professors, and religious/spiritual leaders.

It truly makes my heart sing to see such massive amounts of healing, teamwork, and dedication from people and professionals from all walks of life, and from across the world, who are committed to sharing resources, as well as their knowledge and experience, and supporting others. Every single one of us has a different piece to this puzzle, and when we come together, that's when understanding and healing truly starts to happen. And while the pain of abuse can make people feel profoundly alone, I've found that when that pain is shared, important conversations are opened up, and with that comes a great unifying ability that transcends gender, nationality, religion, sexual orientation, economic status, and/or educational level—and serves to bring us closer together as people in ways that perhaps nothing else could.

Notes

(Endnotes)

1   https://www.ptsd.va.gov/public/ptsd-overview/basics/symp-toms_of_ptsd.asp

Additional Resources

https://www.psychiatry.org/patients-families

https://www.alice-miller.com

https://www.justice.gov/ovw/domestic-violence

https://www.nimh.nih.gov/health/topics/index.shtml

http://ncadv.org/learn-more/statistics

Glossary

Dana Morningstar

Start Here

83119475R00157

Made in the USA
San Bernardino, CA
21 July 2018